AF480622

WELCOME TO INDIA

A Land Of Belonging

Dr. Kinnari Birla-Bharucha

DEDICATION

To the Asian Indian Community worldwide and future generations: let us persist in taking the lead, making a lasting impact on a global scale, and wholeheartedly embracing our Indian heritage.

To all the dedicated allies, the Indian community extends appreciation for your unwavering and continuous support. Thank you.

ACKNOWLEDGMENT

Life, a tapestry woven with purpose, has introduced me to various souls, each shaping my journey. Gratitude overflows to those who've etched their influence on my story, guiding my growth. Every encounter, be it a mentor, a challenger, or a confidant, has enriched my knowledge, skill, and character—a heartfelt nod to everyone walking beside me, shaping my identity and this very book.

Foremost, my late father, Dr. Omprakash Birla, is an enduring presence in my heart. More than a father, he was my guide, strength, and spiritual anchor. His belief in me, his unwavering encouragement, and his ethos of "love all, serve all" have illuminated my path. His legacy of resilience and boundless love for India ignited the spark for my inaugural book, a homage to India's greatness.

My mother, a beacon of strength and grace, has sculpted me into the resilient woman I am. Her sacrifices, tenacity, and nurturing spirit have imprinted on me the essence of motherhood. Her selflessness and wisdom continue to inspire my journey.

Meet my children, Meera and Rayan, the unassuming architects of my character. Their time, patience, and gratitude lessons echo through my daily life, molding my values. They epitomize the true essence of love.

Vaikunth Bharucha, my husband, my partner, my champion in realizing my aspirations. His unswerving dedication, ambition, and unwavering support fuel my pursuits. He is the epitome of stability and focus.

A salute to my brother, a source of unwavering support and unwavering laughter. His empathy, camaraderie, and steadfast presence are my anchors through life's tides.

I also admire my older sister's leadership, hard work, efficiency, strength, determination, and embodiment of community and Indian traditions. Her parental role during our assimilation into the US is forever appreciated.

Family, the cornerstone of my existence, forms the backdrop of my journey. Every soul, from grandparents to cousins, has left an indelible mark on shaping my narrative. Their support and shared moments color my world.

Friends, my chosen family, breathe life into my days. Distances fade as our bond endures, reminding me of life's shared laughter and joys.

Colleagues, mentors, and educators have cultivated my competence and are instrumental in my growth. Their trust and opportunities have shaped my journey.

To my children's caregivers and every individual who's nurtured my children, I extend heartfelt thanks. Your care empowers me to thrive in my endeavors.

My patients, well-wishers, and global Indian communities inspire me with their diverse stories, a testament to life's richness.

To Lincoln Writes, I'm indebted for crafting my ideas into this book. Editorial support, marketing prowess, and publishing expertise have birthed this creation—gratitude to Mr. Alvin Davis for sharing my passion and making my dream a reality.

Above all, I'm humbled by the grace of God and the countless hands that have shaped this project.

ABOUT THE AUTHOR

Born and raised in Gujarat, India, Dr. Kinnari Birla-Bharucha's journey transformed when she and her siblings moved to California in 1992. Currently in Houston, Texas, at forty, she shares her life with her husband and two children, Meera and Rayan. Balancing her Indian heritage with American culture, Dr. Birla-Bharucha has seamlessly integrated these worlds, a wisdom she imparts to her children and readers.

Through "Welcome to India," Dr. Birla-Bharucha sparks pride in Indians worldwide, celebrating India's beauty and heritage and fostering belonging. This book introduces India's culture to others, inviting a sense of connection.

Beyond her roles as mother and wife, Dr. Birla-Bharucha is a dedicated psychologist, caring for patients with combat-related PTSD, depression, and more. Her compassionate care brings hope and joy, extending to her community involvement and leisure pursuits.

Dr. Kinnari Birla-Bharucha

https://twitter.com/BirlaDoc

https://www.instagram.com/dr.birla09/

https://www.facebook.com/profile.php?id=100087045185725

https://docbirla.com/

PREFACE

From the might of the everlasting mountains of the Great Himalayas in the North to the hustle and bustle of Mumbai's metropolis on the West Coast, overlooking the Bay of Bengal—India is a juggernaut of geographical, religious, cultural, and ethnic diversity.

Journey alongside me as we drift gently through the great Ganges, exploring and tasting this diversity to the fullest as the river connects us to each corner of this vast and mystical land.

Let us cross the delicate fabrics of time as we venture through the history that brought us this great nation: from the Indus Valley civilization to the mighty Mughals to the British Raj and to 15th August 1947—the Indian independence.

Feel the tantalizing taste of *Vada Pav* and *Pani Puri* on the tip of your tongue as we walk through the shimmery streets of the metropolises. Feel your nerves relaxing as you take a deep breath in, taking in the serenity of the temples, the gardens, and the architectural magnificence.

Feel free to bring your mental camera along and be ready to ask as many questions as you want because, on this journey, you will witness India in its raw and imperfectly-perfect state. Stay tuned!

CHAPTER 1:

WELCOME TO INDIA

Wherever you are on this Third Rock from the Sun, I wish to teleport you to a place. I'm sure that you must be aware of the term "equator." If you are not, the equator is an imaginary line that crosses through the earth's center.

Regardless of what comes to your mind, I want you to close your eyes and imagine the equator. Imagine standing at the center of that line and then looking to your left, creating an image of vast plains.

Over these plains, imagine buildings and industries and vehicles and bustling streets and smoke and dust. Look to your right and think about all things serene: the brilliant curvature of mountains, valleys, lush green flora, crystalline lakes, and gushing rivers.

Turn around and look ahead. Imagine a vast, unforgiving desert: tall dunes, sand storms, bright, scorching sun, camels, and scorpions and cactuses. Now face North and look straight ahead.

Imagine the relentlessness of the sea: high and low tides, waves, the deep and shallow, fishes and mangroves, and coral reefs.

Whatever you are picturing right now, in some way or the other, you are standing at the center of the equatorial line, and what you are imagining, all around you, is a depiction of "Bharat"—India.

If you are a person who thinks that you live in a culturally and physically diverse region, chances are that you have not been to India.

Every aspect of India, from its ethnicities to its cultures to its geography, is a plethora. If we talk about religion alone, on paper, around seven religions exist throughout the nation—Hinduism, Islam, Christianity, Judaism, Sikhism, Jainism, Buddhism, and Zoroastrianism. But even within these religions, multiple sects and castes exist, like threads of a woven piece of silk.

Similarly, there is the existence of multiple ethnicities, cultures and cultural practices, and sexual and gender identities. Likewise, this diversity is seen in the very tongues of the people who inhabit this land.

Over 122 languages are spoken throughout India, with the mainstream being English, Hindi, Panjabi, Marathi, and Gujarati. This diversity exists even in what people consume. Often outside of India, the food from this region is regarded as "Indian" food. This is a slightly false assumption because, within India, the delicacies enjoyed vary across the land, depending on people, regions, and the cultures in question.

To put all of this into a better perspective, let us understand India from a factual point of view. The nation is located in South Asia and is bordered by Pakistan from the West, China, Nepal, and Bhutan from the North, the Indian Ocean from the South, and the Arabian Sea from the South West.

It is the seventh largest country in the world and the second most populous one. To put this in a better frame, India has an area of almost 3.3 million square kilometers and stretches to about 3300 kilometers from North to South and nearly 3000 kilometers from East to West. The country is very fashionably located in a central position in South Asia, making it an important political, security, and geographical stronghold.

This is because India's position in the geographical sphere of the world gives it access to, and thereby influences, key stakeholders of Asia. These especially include Afghanistan and Pakistan to the West. It also gives it a keen proximity to the Middle East, making it more accessible to countries such as the Kingdom of Saudi Arabia and the United Arab Emirates, which are technological marvels in the current world.

The presence of the Indian Ocean enables connection to countries far off towards the Western hemisphere of the world, namely, the United States of America. The presence of this ocean means huge strides in trade and communication and an influx of imports and exports.

The country's unique position over the equator means it enjoys all five seasons of the world. Although this might not seem like an important factor to the people living there, it holds huge significance in the eyes of the countries to the West, which almost always go through the strides of winter and autumn. India's geographical location is also important because it is located in one of the most nutrient-rich regions of the world. India is blessed with untapped natural resources such as coal, natural gas, and other minerals. Partially explored reserves are spread out in the coal mines of the Jharkhand state.

As per the Energy Information Administration of the United States of America, by 2020, India had an estimated crude oil reserve of around one billion barrels. Huge oil reserves are also located in the offshore fields to the West of Mumbai, and private companies are also involved in oil excavation over the Krishna Godavari Basin. India also made further strides in enhancing their natural resources reserves when their first nuclear power plant, the RAPP-1, started operating in Rajhastan. Knowing that nuclear power exists in South Asia further strengthens India's geographical importance. Apart from this, the plateaus of the region are also rich in minerals such as gold, silver, copper, manganese, and salt.

One of the world's largest natural water resources, the Indus River system, flows through India, and two of its major tributaries, namely, Sutlej and Beas, are also located here. These tributaries are a major resource in India's farming and agricultural business, and naturally, their exports of cotton, rice, and wheat (among other staples) depend on them.

Furthermore, the presence of these tributaries is also important for India's general dominance in the region. Since these tributaries flow through the country, India controls them as they flow into other countries, such as Pakistan. Over this dominance, the Indus Water Treaty was signed between India and Pakistan to settle their disputes over the river and its water allocation. Moreover, the presence of the Indian Ocean towards the South grants India a huge business of fisheries since the Southern strip of the region is enriched with mangroves. This also denotes the environmental importance of the nation as well as the role it plays in the sustainability of the world's natural resources.

However, the abovementioned details are just a summary of what this book entails. This book aims to take the reader through the history of India before coming to its geographical and sociopolitical importance. In my perspective, history is significant because it gives us insights into why India is as important of a region as the world portrays it to be. It aims to take the reader through the period of colonization of India to put into perspective just how important this region was (and is) to foreign powers that they went as far as to colonize the population for almost two centuries. It aims to also take the reader through the era of pre-colonization when the Mughals ruled and, later on, discusses the wave of nationalization that spread among Indians and the seeds that were sown by it that led to its partition. It also aims to discuss, in detail, the era post-partition in India and how, today, in the modern world, it holds a key position from a social, political, geographical, and technological perspective. It will provide insights into one of India's biggest and most important cities of India and how they are significant from a historical and trade perspective, and how they add to the country's Gross Domestic Product (GDP).

I think it is best to set the pace of this book by mentioning two quotes by Mark Twain on the important position of India in the world:

Welcome To India

"India is the cradle of the human race, the birthplace of human speech, the mother of history, the grandmother of legend, and the great-grandmother of tradition. Our most valuable and most instructive materials in the history of man are treasured up in India only."

and

"India is the One land that all men desire to see, and having seen once, by even a glimpse, would not give that glimpse for all the shows of all the rest of the globe combined."

Such is its global importance.

CHAPTER 2:

ANCESTORS

India is not a monolith.
It is incredibly diverse.

By that, I mean that unlike many other places in the world that exist with one culture that has been present in their respective geographical area for millennia, India is a culmination of different cultures that became intertwined in this region of South Asia throughout history and created what we call the Indian culture of today. Millennia of rich history have amalgamated in this region –from functioning as a conduit through Asia to allowing itself to become a breeding ground for innovation and change, to the immense years upon years of diversity among the kind of rulers it had over hundreds of years— India can never be considered a monolith.

If you think of Russia, you think of the Russians. When you think of Norway, you think of the Norwegians; you can not do the same for India. India has the Panjabis, the Tamils, the descendants of hundreds of other ethnicities that emigrated from different parts of the world and made India theirs, thus allowing themselves to become Indians then themselves. Their culture became Indian, and they became Indian, as India took from them and became India as we know it today.

The place has been the hallmark of interdisciplinary practices, traditions, languages, food, and much more.

And so I think it would be unfair, or uninformed at least, to understand this place from one lens or one point of view. You need to eat the food item and all of them. It would help if you met different people—all of them. You need to swim the waters and visit the temples, mosques, and all the other sites that show you the history of this vast land and the people that exist, have existed and will continue to exist. You might have to become Indian and spend the rest of your life trying to understand what India is.

The real India.

India has worlds inside itself, and they can not be seen in a touristy and gimmicky manner.

The Real India is what drove me to write this book in the first place, if I may add.

Hence, to truly understand India and its overabundance of practices, cultures, beliefs, and religions, it is only fair to go back in time and visit its ancestral history.

Remember, you are still standing in the center of the equator.

I now want you to close your eyes again and imagine yourself sitting in the pilot seat of a time machine, fiddling with buttons and gauges around you. You must now set your desired period to be 5000 years before today. You must now click whatever button will warp the fabric of time and speed.

Open your eyes again; you are now 5000 years into the past.

Somewhere around you, there is the Indus Valley civilization. You are now witnessing, in some ways, the birth of Indus Civilization as you stand in a place that roughly existed 2500 years before the birth of Christ.

Throughout this history of 5000 years, we will see one constant element flowing seamlessly through the chambers of time. This element is the River Indus, the river around which the entirety of the Indus Valley civilization was based; it was also the cause of their demise, making the civilization all the more interesting and tragic.

The river flows through modern-day north-western India, and some of its major tributaries flow into modern-day Pakistan and enter the regions of Punjab until they eventually flow into the Arabian Sea.

In this region of Punjab, one of the civilization's major cities, Harappa, existed near the Indus tributary called River Ravi. As we follow the river's course into the region of Sindh in Pakistan, we will come across the other major city of this civilization, Moenjo Daro. This method of following the river was a literal practice of modern-day archaeologists as they attempted to uncover the secrets of the Indus Valley civilization. To their surprise, this method yielded exceptional results as the sub-parts of the civilization, consisting of more than 100 cities, were starting to reveal all around the river's course.

The investigations of said archaeologists have revealed that the people of the Indus Valley civilization were descendants of the Mesopotamian civilization, and hence it is only natural that they picked up on certain ways of Ancient Mesopotamia. This was most evident in their methods of agriculture.

They were mostly dependent on skilled methods of irrigation to water their crops.

They had also mastered the skill of timing their crops so that they made the best use of the devastating annual floods of the River Indus. These floods left the nearby basin land covered with alluvium, rich in minerals, and healthy for a good crop yield. The main crops they grew consisted of wheat, barley, field peas, mustard, sesame, and dates, and some of the earliest traces of cotton were also uncovered by researchers. Animals were an integral part of the Indus Valley civilization, especially because of their use as livestock. Evidence uncovered by archaeologists suggested the presence of domesticated animals such as dogs, cats, cattle, buffaloes, and possibly pigs. Remains of ivory tusks were also found, which indicates the possibility of domesticating Asian elephants.

The political structure and system of the Indus Valley remain a matter of debate through this day; however, throughout major cities, there was an evident difference in the sizes and types of houses present there, which suggested some form of class divide, and wherever there is a class divide, one can infer that some form of capitalism could have existed in the system of economics and governance. This is not an unnatural theory either, as trade was a major part of the economy of the civilization.

The unveiling and unearthing of the cities of Moenjo Daro and Harappa by archaeologists showed a huge degree of uniformity in the material objects or culture present in the two cities, which suggests a great degree of internal trade. The presence of multiple valuable minerals that were uncovered suggested that the Indus state was part of a deep trade network because such minerals were not indigenous. Gold that was found was most certainly exported from areas of northern Karnataka. Lapiz Lazuli could have possibly been imported from Iran. Lead and copper could have arrived from places such as Rajhastan. Regardless, it was well established that the Indus Valley civilization had contacts spread out to different sub-continent areas through trade.

However, what the Indus Valley civilization would perhaps be best known for and the one thing that would continue its influence in generations to follow would be their take on artifacts and artwork. Their best local work included seals made from soapstone, over which they performed carvings to depict various scenes. These would often show animals such as elephants, tigers, and bulls carved from a copper tool. There is much conjecture over the use of these seals because while many considered them to have religious connotations, others argued that they were used as nothing more than but means of trade. Many researchers often categorize them under amulets. Regardless of their nature, one cannot disagree that they showed high craftsmanship.

The blacksmith industry of the civilization was also quite significant. Many daily-use objects such as chisels, knives, pots, and spearheads were made of melting metals such as gold and copper. They are believed to be made from the simple casting, chiseling, and hammering processes.

It is not surprising that the civilization lasted for a long time because there was some degree of order and uniformity in the way they functioned, and this can be seen in the very example of their script because, throughout the cities of the Indus state, one can see the presence of Harappan script which shows that a uniform way of writing was implemented throughout the civilization. However, towards the end of it, this uniformity of it was slowly starting to erode.

This happened on a physical scale, and towards the end cycle of the civilization, the cities were hit by devastating floods whose after-affects were uncovered by modern archaeologists. This obviously sowed some seeds of economic and social decline, but the end of the civilization is usually marked by the end of its main city, Moenjo Daro, which was sudden and is still unclear. Many suggest that a flash flood eroded the city, while others argue that it was attacked by Indo-European raiders who left a pile of bodies behind.

Again, regardless of the nature of things, many parts of the culture and the lifestyle of the Indus Valley civilization are now enunciated in the Indian culture as well, which is only natural because of the geographical setting of the area.

Since the Indus Valley civilization mainly lies in modern-day Pakistan and India, we can find the presence of the civilization's marks all over India's arts and crafts, especially in the way that Indian agriculture is still practiced.

CHAPTER 3:

THE GREAT MUGHALS

The history of India would be incomplete without the Mughals. If we could return to our time machine, we would visit South Asia towards the end of the 16th century. This was when Babur, the first Mughal Emperor, invaded India. Unbeknownst to all, the Mughals were never the inherent rulers of India or the subcontinent. They too, were invaders.

Babur belonged to the regions of central Asia, and Mongolian blood ran through his veins. His ancestry was something that drove his interest in South Asia. He was a descendant of Timur and the great Genghis Khan. Towards the late 16th century, he established his base in Kabul, Afghanistan, and drove into the subcontinent through the timeless Khyber pass. His forces defeated Ibrahim Lodi's in the first Battle of Panipat, and after a series of definitive victories, thus began the Mughal rule over the subcontinent. However, his short reign over the empire was marked with instability, and eventually, his son, Humayun, the second Mughal emperor, took over in around 1530. Like his father, his rule was also marked with instability, and it came to the point that after losing a huge amount of land to the Pashtuns under the leadership of Sher Shah Suri, he was exiled by his people to Persia. In Persia, he formulated a greater empire, and after 15 years, he took control of the land that was once his again. It was through his invasion that Persian art, architecture, culture, and language entered India as well. The end of his reign marked the beginning of his son Akbar's, who is regarded as the Greatest Mughal Emperor ever to live.

Akbar was as efficient of a ruler as he was a military commander. In his reign, he consolidated most of northern and central India under his map. He was also known for his liberal attitude toward life and leadership. He was a curious man, especially on matters of religion, and that is why his courts consisted of many Muslim, Hindu, and Buddhist scholars who would debate the sincerity of each of their respective faiths. It was also known that Akbar created his religion, ce at one point Eventually, he gave up practicing his faith and reverted to Islam.

While ruling an empire as large as the one that he had, Akbar was also making sure that he was sowing the right seeds for the next of his kin to take over. Since two of his sons died in infancy, he ensured that his third son Humayun received the right brought up and education to take over the throne eventually. When Jahangir took over, he did not disappoint. He was responsible for doing something that his father never could. He ended the century-long struggle of the Mughals with the Rajput as he pushed them to such an extent that they eventually had to surrender their lives and property. He also managed to take over the fort of Kangra, something Akbar had always dreamed of doing. However, his health was severely compromised because of his drinking habits, and he died in 1627, and his son Khurram took his throne and henceforth regarded himself as "Shah Jehan."

Shah Jehan is perhaps best known for his architectural feats as he is associated with monumental buildings of the subcontinent, such as the Great Taj Mahal that he built in memory of his late wife, the Red Fort in Delhi, the Wazir Khan Mosque and the Moti Masjid in Lahore. When Shah Jehan fell ill in 1657, his late wife Mumtaz's eldest son, Dara, took control of his responsibilities; however, his other sons, namely Aurangzeb, Shuja, and Murad, marched over to Agra, defeated Dara's forces, and took over their share. They collectively chose Aurangzeb as the leader of the Mughals, and this began his reign—and perhaps the rule of the final Mughal emperor.

Aurangzeb's entire reign was almost marked with warfare as he started a program of military expansion. Although he was successful in his attempts, and the empire grew to regions of modern-day Afghanistan in the North West and Bijapur in the South, the sheer vastness of the kingdom, the depleting treasury, and Aurangzeb's religious intolerance meant that the chain of command throughout his region became weaker. His empire ended in a frenzy as it broke down into factions towards its end as Aurangzeb tried to control rebellions started by the Pashtuns, the Sikhs, and the Marathas.

Although the empire spanned over the lifetime of five different emperors, its administrative nuances can somewhat be summarized. The legal system, for example, evolved through the rule of various emperors, but since all of them were Muslim, the system did see the interpretation of the Islamic *Fiqh* (or the rule of law) being applied to it. This included using *Muftis* (religious scholars) and implementing rules and regulations in the light of the Qur'an: the Holy Book of Islam.

The economy of the Mughals was vast and prosperous; however, one of the most important feats they could achieve was that they standardized their currency to the rupee and dam (copper coins) used throughout their empire. Their general administrative mode of rule was not unrecognized to us. It consisted of dividing the territory into provinces and appointing governors for each. Similarly, different departments of administration were also established with someone to look over each, for example, the treasury, the military, and the finance department. All these departments, in turn, reported to the emperor.

One can assign various reasons for the general decline of the vast Mughal Empire, but there is one that stands out always. That reason existed in the shadows and merely waited and watched while the empire crumbled in front of them, and they swept in at just the right time. This reason is the arrival of the British, who stepped into the lands during the reign of Shah Jehan in 1615. They arrived as traders under the East India Company, and after achieving their purpose of establishing a trading route to India, they were overwhelmed by the massive wealth the empire held. This glitter urged them to play their long-standing game as they slowly started interfering with Mughal policies and politics. Their long-standing game eventually unraveled after more than 200 years of colonial rule.

CHAPTER 4:

ENTER THE BRITISH

The decline of the Mughal empire has always been a questionable point for historians. Many argue that the general dynamics of the empire were the reason that led to their inevitable downfall. This includes multiple factors: the vastness of the kingdom, which made it difficult to administer, the nationalist uprisings in different areas of the region, and religious intolerance, to name a few. However, there is one external factor that all historians agree to as one of the biggest (and hidden) reasons for the downfall of this great dynasty: the arrival of the British.

As mentioned earlier, the British arrived in the subcontinent under the name of the East India Company, and, indeed, from the beginning, it can be inferred that their interests were solely trading-related. Only when they became exposed to the sheer wealth of India did they realize that it led to the eventual annexation. Their initial motive for moving into India was because they wanted to break into the profitable spice trade of the East Indies, which was being enjoyed by the Dutch, the Spanish, and the Portuguese, and, as mentioned earlier, they were granted the permit to trade in India by Emperor Shah Jehan in 1612 officially. This began their slow but sure move into Indian politics and administration.

The company itself was formed in 1600 to break into South East Asia's silk and spice trade. It was granted a trading charter by the Queen herself in 1600. Over time it gained many other names, as discussed below, but its basic purpose remained the same. It eventually became the mode of the establishment of British imperialism in India.

Initially, the company settled down to trade cotton, silk, indigo, and spices. They later established a very profitable (and exploitative) chain of trade in indigo in the regions of Bengal. This was because indigo was a popular trading plant for the British because of the vast profits it gave them in Britain. The profits existed because of the popularity of indigo used in British cloth manufacturing industries as a dye. Since indigo was not grown in England, the subcontinent became a valuable resource for harboring it.

The greatest example of the company's unfair trading practices is how they handled indigo with the Indians. They exploited the farmers and the landowners (the *zamindars*) by striking fraudulent deals with them. The basic method that they employed was the following. They obviously could not take over control of a piece of land that a farmer-owned, so they made a deal with them wherein they would give them loans in advance to buy all the necessary material required to grow indigo. When indigo was to be cultivated at the end of the year, their deal solely relied on whether profit was achieved. This meant that the British would take over all the plantation that was produced, but if there were not a surplus in production, they would incur a debt against the farm owner's name. Since the margin of "surplus" in crop growth is not a constant one, over time, these debts started to grow, and it came to the point that the farm owners were under an indefinite obligation with their foreign investors. Of course, the investors still ensured that they gave them enough capital for plantations in the following year, but they always cut a certain margin from it because of the debt. This meant that a surplus in production was virtually impossible, leaving the landowners in an unpayable situation. This would eventually lead to the famous Indigo Revolt of Bengal in 1859.

The company was also known for using slave labor from Indonesia, West Africa, and East Africa which were transported to their holdings in India. They were especially known to traffic slaves from areas such as Mozambique and Madagascar, already under British colonial rule by then, and transported ships to their holdings in places such as India. By the mid 18th century, the cotton trade had started declining, and the company began importing goods from China and selling them opium. Opium trade with China grew vastly at this time because the East India Company needed the money to finance its purchases of Indian tea, spices, silk, and other goods. Eventually, there came opposition from the Chinese to their opium trade which led to the first Opium War fought in 1839, in which the Chinese faced defeat which increased British trading privileges. Their trading privilege was firmly established, and simultaneously the Chinese control of the Opium trade was lost when they saw another defeat at the hands of the British in the Second Opium war in 1860.

But it was not just the external forces that threatened the expansion of EIC (East India Company). It was also their own people. The original company faced much opposition from the capitalists of Britain due to its monopoly, which led to the formation of a rival company and, eventually, the fusion of the two into the United Company of Merchants of England trading to the East Indies.

While their initial motive for entering India was spice trading, they soon started getting involved in other side missions that were a direct cause of their increased influence. But they could involve themselves in other businesses while being in someone else's territory through their power. When EIC stepped into India and obtained permission to trade from the local Mughal authorities, they started ensuring that they were in the "good light" of the locals by getting involved in duty-free, mutually beneficial trade. Soon they used their influence to get permits from authorities to hold lands that firmly established their holdings. The effect of this became extremely evident when they started using these holdings to get involved in territorial and control-based hostilities with rival European companies, in which they used local Indian soldiers that they had hired to work for them. It is also important to note that at this point, it was not the East India Company that was conducting these rivalries; it was the British government itself because by the late 1700s, after passing a series of India Acts, they had virtually taken control of the company and any land that came under it. This meant that when the British executed, their military might overthrow the Nawab of Bengal, it meant that one of the largest independent states of the subcontinent was now under British rule, and they had essentially established a puppet of the British government in India in 1757 with this annexation.

But the British control of Bengal did not just come in the colloquial way mentioned above. The actions of the East India Company itself led to the British taking control over the administration of Bengal from them. When the company itself gained control of Bengal, they were blinded by the vast area they had under him and the riches it contained. Soon, they indulged in a huge degree of mismanagement under the lust for self-indulgence. They involved themselves in a massive tax look where the farmers and landowners were exploited to the point that an enormous famine struck Bengal in 1770. This directly affected the company as well because due to their own actions, their revenue from Bengal fell immensely, leading to them appealing for an emergency loan of 1 million pounds to avoid bankruptcy. The British government obliged because they did not want such a productive region to be lost from under their noses, so they bailed the company out. However, even the Crown itself was ashamed at the huge degree of mismanagement that prevailed in Bengal as it directly reflected on the British government itself, and that is when they decided to pass the Regulation Act of 1773, where they started overseeing the management of EIC in Bengal. They followed this by passing the India Act of 1784, with which they officially took administrative control and control of the political policy of the Indian regions under the East India Company.

But here comes a big question that one might ask. How does a foreign company that stepped into the lands of the subcontinent start simply grabbing lands that did not belong to them? Well, the simple answer to that question is that, in some ways, they were enabled. By the early 1800s, the East India Company had an army comprising around 200,000 soldiers on foot to defend their outposts. This army (along with their superior military might) enabled their way of taking over lands, but the game they played was slow. Initially, they entered into trade agreements with royal states, and later, they used these very armies to threaten these states, renegotiate taxation laws, and enforce ruinous taxation, which essentially allowed them to collect taxes from farmers and landowners alike. In simple words, it was legal and sanctioned looting on their behalf. Later, the might of these very armies was used to annex land.

Over the next nine decades until the First War of Independence of India, the British established direct control over India through wars, treaties, and annexations. Where they could not simply grab lands, they used their influence to develop mutually beneficial treaties with the rulers of such states. They merely took control of socio-politically unstable areas with their military might. Thus spread the dominion of the British over India under the shadow of the East India Company.

CHAPTER 5:

WAR OF INDEPENDENCE

The details mentioned in the preceding chapter foregrounded everything to come next. Now close your eyes as I take you through this journey—the journey of the perils of the Indian people living under British dominion after the late 1700s. Imagine the following sceneries in vivid detail because they would go on to become major causes from the breakout of the first Indian War of Independence in 1857.

By the late 18th century, the British had infiltrated almost every administrative sector of India and essentially ruled the subcontinent under technicalities. One could argue that the role of princes remained important in this time, but in reality, these princes subjugated themselves to the will of the white man because they feared oppression. The British constantly expanded their political control under their "divide and conquer" policy. These became evident under blatant policies introduced by them. The most famous and enraging bhas the Doctrine of Lapse, introduced by Lord Dalhousie. Under this rule of law, the British did not even bother hiding their nature of annexation—it was too blatantly obvious. It states that if any Hindu prince responsible for a state died without a natural heir, their land would be annexed by the British administration. In this way, areas such as Jaitpur, Sambalpur, Baghat, and Udaipur, to name a few, came under British control. This enticed hatred among the Indian Hindus, but their treatment of the Mughal emperors particularly triggered Indian Muslims because they were an important symbol of Muslim power for them. They declared that they would abolish the title of "Mughal Emperor" after the death of Bahadur Shah Zafar (often regarded as the last true Mughal emperor) and take over his palace and fort.

Political control was not the only reason the Indian Hindus were enraged by British rule. When the British took over the administration, they replaced old methods of government with their own "Rule of Law," which was not met with appreciation. Furthermore, British control of administration meant that most Indians could not adopt higher posts in the government, and those who already had high posts soon found themselves unemployed. Those with posts in the administration faced severe discrimination regarding the pay gap. Indians who worked at the same posts as the British and worked the same hours realized they were severely underpaid compared to their white counterparts. It soon became evident that they were not treated as counterparts; they were seen as inferiors by their foreign masters. Their administrative control also meant that traditional values that Hindus and Muslims relied on, such as the *Dharmshastra* system and the *Shariah*, were no longer applicable on a larger scale which the locals did not appreciate. This discrimination regarding adopting posts was felt in every administration sector, including the military. Naturally, the Indians felt exploited because they were excluded from privileges in their land.

Perhaps one of the most frustrating factors for the locals was how their wealth was being managed. It is famously said that the British treated India like a sponge, wherein they soaked all the wealth from India (including their heritage) and squeezed it all into Britain, creating a massive pool of wealth which the locals were excluded from. The British trade policies completely obliterated the subcontinent's agricultural industry, leaving one thriving country as a poor one. In short, the Indian agricultural sector became the production line of raw materials to be fed to the Industrial revolution of manufactured goods in Britain.

The Indians also felt that the British stepped out of bounds regarding their social and religious reforms. They treated the Indians like an inferior race, so they thought that every religious and social practice they disagreed with or offended them needed to be banned. This was evident in their treatment of the intersex community of the subcontinent, which was once a community of extreme importance and high regard in the Mughal courts. The British felt the need to mistreat non-procreative sexualities. They went as far as to label them as a criminal tribe in 1871 under Section 377 of the Indian Penal Code. Their religious intolerance was felt when they banned certain cultural practices of Hindus and Muslims. They banned Sati and child marriage, to name a few, and these were met with hatred from the communities affected by this cultural overstep. They also felt that intrusions were being done on their religious practices on the grounds of Christianity because this time became allegedly famous for conversions to Christianity, and the Religious Disabilities Act that was passed in 1856 decided that people would not be deprived of their hereditary rights on properties on the grounds of changing religions; this was also seen as a means to increase the popularity of Christianity.

But perhaps the most important cause of the War of Independence of 1857 was the military disparity between the British and Indians. These seeds acted as poison, slowly seeping into the grounds until they polluted the entire land and eventually sparked the war in a flash. These started with general concerns of the Indians. The British were known to look down upon Indian soldiers despite the heavy numbers in their army. They were paid low salaries and were not promoted above the rank of *"subedar."* They were extremely grieved by the General Service Enlistment Act of 1856, which dictated that Indian soldiers could be posted anywhere overseas in the British Empire. Many sepoys considered traveling outside of their lands to be an encroachment on their religious beliefs, but, more importantly, their lack of consent in this entire proposition is what struck them because they had to move away from their families and loved ones on the grounds of an Act, they had no say on. They were enraged at the Crown's general annexation practices as well, and they were particularly struck at the unfair annexation of Awadh because a huge number of soldiers in the British army were from Awadh. The soldiers were asked to fight in wars started by the British in far-off lands, but they were not given any special privileges, paid any compensation, or any medallion of honor for their duties and sacrifices.

However, the trigger to all of this came as mere Enfield rifles. The British introduced these new rifles to the army, which required tearing open the cartridge with one's teeth to load it. However, Hindus and Muslims found this practice unacceptable because the cartridges were coated with pig and cow fat. Hindus considered cows sacred, while Muslims were forbidden from consuming pigs. This caused multiple sepoys to resist, and their aftermath angered the Indians and led to the war.

In March 1857, in Barrackpore, a sepoy named Mangal Pandey refused to obey British orders and attacked his superior officers, leading to his arrest and execution in April. This news spread like wildfire, and in late April, sepoy troops at Meerut refused to cooperate, and they were arrested and given long-term sentences. This, eventually, spirited their comrades to revolt against their superiors in May, and they, henceforth, shot British officers and marched off to Delhi, where there was no foreign control.

Here the troops joined the local sepoy garrison, and together they empowered the aged Mughal Emperor Bahadur Shah Zafar II to take control and restore their power in Delhi. However, the effort was an extremely scattered one. Most of the royal states were still loyal to the British, and only the old Mughal emperor and his sons, along with Nana Sahib in the north, took part in the effort. This meant that the British soon overcame the effort as they led campaigns around the regions of Lucknow between 1857 and 1858 led by Sir Colin Campbell, and, eventually, the movement led by Sir Hugh Rose in early 1858 came to declare an end to the supposed war. There was mutiny associated on both sides of the campaign as the Indian soldier shot their British superiors and, in return, the British became responsible for mass massacres in the regions of Delhi and Kanpur as hundreds of sepoys were fired from canons in the frenzy of British rage.

There were several aftermaths of the war. A financial burden was put on the British government in their efforts to overcome Indian resistance, which led to them reorganizing Indian finances and the army. It was all part of their divide-and-rule campaign. However, one seemingly positive outcome of the war was that the Indians had shown their resistance to foreign control to some extent which made the British understand that they were better off including Indians in administrative decisions regarding them rather than keeping them on the sidelines; hence, the new Legislative Council of 1861 allowed Indian representation. Obviously, this representation's strength, role, and actual power were minimal, so it did not have much effect. However, historians often interpret the failure of the Indian resistance as an official establishment of the Western class system over the subcontinent which led to the birth of a strong (and spiteful) middle class of Indians that was spirited with a sense of nationalism (hence establishing the roots for Indian independence of 1947). The after-effects of the war, especially the birth of nationalist ideas, are well reflected in the literature that followed this era, especially in the works of the Progressive Writers of the early 1900s.

One interesting aspect of the war depends a lot on the observer's perspective. For the Indians, it was a matter of resistance, a rebellion against their alien oppressors. Hence, they labeled it as the Indian War of Independence of 1857. For the colonizers themselves, it was a riot, so their interpretation of the effort is always marked with either the term "riot" or "mutiny."

@btushar02

CHAPTER 6:

OUR LAND

India truly was the land of the Indians, and it belonged to them. They had every inherent right over it, not just over it, but over its resources.

But like the sponge analogy mentioned previously, the colonizers had not only stolen these rights from the natives but had ensured that they soaked all possible wealth they could from the subcontinent and brought it back to their native land.

This treasure is still displayed in museums as a relic of Great Britain's past when it is the heritage they stole from the lands they colonized.

Their oppressive regime only strengthened in their acts after the Indian War of Independence in 1857. Their lack of trust in the Indians was only aggravated.

It started with introducing the Government of India Act of 1858, an immediate aftermath of the war. The British blamed the war entirely on the mismanagement of the administration of the East India Company rather than their imperialist practices, and this led to a direct transfer of authoritative powers in the hands of the Crown over the subcontinent.

Although the Crown entrusted the affairs of India to a Secretary of State and their advisory council, actual power remained in the hands of Viceroys who governed India directly.

These viceroys implemented a stronghold of over 1500 Indian Civil Service agents posted throughout British India, and they made sure that the Indians themselves were given as little role in these posts as possible.

When Lord Canning (Viceroy from 1856-62) came into power as Viceroy, he abolished Lord Dalhousie's previous annexation laws and introduced a non-interaction policy with the princely states due to the revolt.

Princes were free to govern their land however they liked if they swore allegiance to the British Crown. They also adopted new policies of religious non-interference out of the fear of another "mutiny" because they were more than aware that the introduction of Christian missionaries and their general interference with Indian religious practices had been a major cause of the riot of 1857.

Their general attitude towards the locals was distrust, indifference, or fear. The viceroys themselves had established huge military towns or camps where they stayed under security and a lavish lifestyle. Their fear of the locals was evident in how they reorganized the army. They increased the ratio of British to Indian soldiers in the army to ensure that there was more of the white man in the military in case of a dispute.

By 1867, a safer mix of 43000 British soldiers and 228000 Indian troops was adopted, and, like before, the Indian forces were discriminated against from adopting higher posts.

Moreover, the Indians couldn't handle "advanced" weapons or machinery. Indians didn't have much input into how they were governed, and any measures introduced by the British were only done to show the Indians were involved, but they weren't very involved.

As mentioned previously, the legislative council was opened to some Indian members, but they barely had a say there.

At this point, the Indians became convinced that there was no true way in which they could work under the oppressive regime of the British.

They realized there was no true way to co-exist with the white man under the "divide and rule" policy.

Through self-determination, they realized they could only put forward their demands and work on a civilized front for the Indians and only the Indians.

To some extent, they found self-determination under the establishment of political parties, namely the Indian National Congress and the Muslim League.

Nationalist ideas had seeped into Indian soil after the Indian War of Independence of 1857, and, as a result, the Indian National Congress first met in December 1885.

Initially, the Congress was a party that represented the needs of all Indians, and it even included prominent Muslim members such as Muhammad Ali Jinnah (who would later join the Muslim League), which showed the united front of the Indians.

It wasn't until the 20th century that a split between the Hindu and Muslim parts of the party became apparent. Most Muslim members wanted higher representation under British rule, while the Hindus had adopted a more *"Swadeshi"* (self-determination) role, and they wanted separation from the British.

It had also become evident to the Muslims that they could never truly put forward their demands for peace under a party that Hindus dominated. This, henceforth, led to the establishment of the All-India Muslim League in 1906 to safeguard the rights of Indian Muslims.

Even though the British supported this division (which is not surprising considering their divide-and-rule policy), the League also adopted a self-governance motto for the Indians by 1913.

By the 1920s, the Congress was led by the famous Mohandas Karamchand "Mahatma" Gandhi, while the Muslim League was led by notable leaders such as Muhammad Ali Jinnah and Liaquat Ali Khan.

By this time, the Congress, under the leadership of Gandhi, had adopted a policy of non-cooperative nonviolence in which they boycotted British goods and encouraged the purchase of Indian manufactured ones.

But both parties didn't have much hope that the British would give them more representation in the government, especially because they had been promised the same thing after Indian locals supported the British for so long.

After the war ended, the British reverted to imperialism. During the infamous *Khilafat* (Caliphate) Movement, the *Khalifa* of Turkey was poorly treated by the British, and the Muslims lost hope too.

Indian nationalism was sowed into Indian culture due to events in this era, particularly how the British treated Indians.

It wasn't uncommon for Indians to think coexistence with foreign masters was possible before this. Still, events after the War of Independence of 1857, especially the British disregard for their Indians in military and administrative matters, made coexistence with foreigners hard.

Consequently, nationalism soared through the skies of India and could be seen in both the agendas of the two biggest political parties in the country, the Indian National Congress and the All-India Muslim League.

CHAPTER 7:

LAHORE RESOLUTION

And so, nationalism had seeped into the deep roots of colonial India, and, as mentioned before, the locals were no longer fooled by the idea of cooperation with their foreign masters.

Despite the locals finding some form of representation under political parties, they knew they could not immediately expect independence. It would take a lot of work and negotiations with their "masters," unwilling to give up the land they had so ruthlessly snatched. And why would they want to?

For them, it was not a matter of the feelings of the Indians. White supremacy was built on the notion that white people had this preconceived notion that it was their destiny to grab these lands and loot them off their riches.

They believed other races, such as Asians, Africans, and Native Americans, were destined to serve them. Such was deep the extent of this mindset. The Indians spent years of colonial rule living under torment and new, unfair administrations while the British fueled their industries and urbanization through the wealth they stole from these lands.

The early 20th century in India, particularly after World War I, was marked by notable events depicting the struggle of the local Indians to demand higher representation from their foreign masters.

Before moving into the turbulent history of the 1930s, it is worth noting that before the start of the decade, the British made vain efforts to get somehow the Indians to cooperate with them. They manifested as a Simon Commission that arrived in India in 1927, a seven-man committee under Sir John Simon.

Immediately, it was boycotted by all major political parties in India because, as usual, it had no Indian representation. It published a two-volume report in 1929 but could hardly expect the Indians to obey the propositions.

March of 1930 arrived, and Gandhi decided that the way to oppose British rule in India was through non-violent non-cooperation. He labeled it under the term *"Satyagraha,"* in which he called out for mass civil disobedience, a practice he had followed when he was protesting the rights of Indians in South Africa.

But this disobedience's target was not just the British rule in India. It was towards the unfair and exorbitant salt taxes that the British had deployed on Indians.

The Salt Act of 1882 dictated that the Indians could no longer collect or harvest salt on their land. Instead, they had to purchase it from British merchants, meaning they had no control over the unfair pricing of such a vital staple in their diet.

And hence, from March to April of 1930, Gandhi gathered a following of over 60,000 Indians as they marched from his religious retreat in Ahmedabad to the Arabian Sea Coast (almost 240 miles), where they planned on harvesting salt from pits.

The British deployed forces there to destroy the pits, which meant that salt could not be harvested in masses, but Gandhi still went on there and grabbed a handful of salt from one of the pits, thereby breaking British law. Many arrests were made, including Gandhi, but the *"Satyagraha"* or the Salt March continued. It was a mass disobedience, one that the British did not expect.

To discuss the findings of the Simon Commission and to increase Indian inclusivity in the political process, in the late 1930s, the British made another effort in vain as they invited the leaders of the major political parties of India to Britain to a conference which became known as the First Round Table Conference of November 1930.

Unfortunately, the Indian National Congress entirely boycotted it, and little progress could be made without any representation from the most influential party of colonial India.

However, relations between Gandhi and the government eased off a little as Gandhi signed a pact with the new viceroy, Lord Irwin, in March 1931, stating that he would officially call off the non-cooperation movement and participate in the Second Round Table Conference.

Like the previous one, this too was doomed to fail because weeks before the conference was to be conveyed, the Conservatives had replaced the Labour government, and that meant that the Indians were indicated with a stringent attitude as they arrived at the meeting.

Furthermore, the Indians were divided into factions as Gandhi claimed to represent all of them, while other delegates (especially the ones from the Muslim League) disagreed with him.

One could somewhat predict the trajectory in which the future of India was going from this key event as it could be seen that not only nationalism had spread into the general population of India itself but also throughout different subdivisions.

But the British were too naïve to see this for the clear picture it was. Instead, they convened a Third Round Table Conference in 1933, which was neither attended by the Indian National Congress nor any other major political party in India.

Despite this, the British felt conceited enough to draft the conferences' findings, publish them in a white paper in 1933, and use them to formulate a new constitution for India, introduced in 1935 as the Government of India Act. It was evident to the Indians, especially to the members of the Indian National Congress, that the act was nothing but a means for the British to control their control of colonial India (now under the title of a federation), and it opposed the idea of a *"raj"* proposed by Gandhi, Nehru, and other prominent Indian leaders.

Yet, the Muslim perspective also became extremely important to future events. The Muslims believed that since they were a one-fourth minority in the population of India, they would essentially be living as a prominent minority under the democratic system if the British government granted the concept of Raj to the Indian National Congress. It was not even about Congress, *per se.*

It was mostly related to the fact that in any case of the British granting joint independence to the Indians, since Muslims were a minority, they believed they would find themselves at a disadvantage.

Throughout major conferences of the 1930s, the Muslims, to protect their social, political, cultural, and religious rights, kept demanding separate electorates for separate identities. However, they eventually concluded that separate electorates alone would not be enough to safeguard their rights.

Muhammad Iqbal, the famous Muslim philosopher and poet, made his famous address in Allahabad, which made it clear that he believed that coexistence with both the Hindus and the British was impossible since Hindus have their methods of governance, as do Muslims.

He sent multiple letters to Mr. Jinnah in which he convinced him that the only true way for the Muslims to secure their rights was by demanding a separate state.

When Jinnah returned to politics in 1939, he received overwhelming support from the Muslim masses in his call to celebrate the Day of Deliverance on 29th December 1939. He had officially become the leader in promoting the rights of the Muslim community in India.

He, henceforth, decided to act on the mission of a separate nation. He called for the 27ᵗʰ annual All India Muslim League session to be held from March 22ⁿᵈ to 24ᵗʰ, 1940, at Lahore, and he informed all the print media that they should expect the Muslim League to release a huge policy change.

The prominent Muslim leaders who attended this meeting included Nawab Bahadur Yar Jang, Barkat Ali, Khawaja Nazimuddin, Qazi Muhammad Isa, I.I. Chundigar, Abdullah Haroon, and many others. The inaugural session was held in Minto Park in Lahore, and the attendance included around 100,000 people, meaning the park was jam-packed by the afternoon.

During this session, Muhammad Ali Jinnah made his famous address to the crowd gathered in front of him in which he claimed that Hindus and Muslims were a separate nation and the idea of coexistence between them was entirely impossible.

He recalled the suffering of the Muslims in the past years, both at the hands of the British and the Hindus, and he declared that regardless of how much Hindus regard themselves as nationalists, at the end of the day, they were Hindus first. On March 23ʳᵈ, the historical Lahore Resolution was released, and it solidified the new policy that the Muslims had adopted towards their foreign masters and the Hindu majority.

It completely rejected the ideals presented by the Government of India Act of 1935 and contended that no revised plan would be accepted without the approval and consent of the Muslims.

It also dictated that any future constitutional plan would only be acceptable to the Muslims if it were based upon the idea that geographically contiguous areas where the Muslims were a majority were to be grouped to constitute independent states which shall be entirely autonomous in their control. It was, in total, a lengthy five-paragraph resolution, but, in simple words, it was calling for the formation of a separate Muslim state. The demands of the Muslims had become clear.

So, by the early 1940s, the demands of the two major parties of British India had become clear. While the Indian National Congress wanted the immediate expulsion of foreign rules from India and the transfer of political control to them, the Muslims wanted to safeguard their rights by forming a separate state away from the Hindus.

One thing had become clear, India had reached its climax of political instability, and it was only a matter of time before something went down. It was now up to the British Crown to react to these demands.

In comes the Second World War.

CHAPTER 8:

SEPARATION AND FREEDOM

When the second World War appeared, it was not anything different for the Indians. It was the same old routine; the actions of the white man and their repercussions being borne by the so-called "subjects."

The war is often seen in the same binary as the white man sees the world, and that is the power of narratives. History is naming, and naming is power, as Michel Truillot would say.

It is often misconstrued as a black-and-white struggle between the Axis and the Allied powers. But this perception always fails to overlook the fact that the Allied powers could never have defeated the Axis forces without the contributions of their colonized states.

In presenting this narrative, a scattered memory remains of the sacrifices of the 2.5 million troops India voluntarily sent—the largest arms force in history.

It was the Raj at war, as much as Great Britain itself. Yet stories are told of the valor of the white man. Tales were told of the tunnelers digging and crawling under Dunkirk's uninhabited land as if only the white man smeared their face with grease and dirt.

The aftermath of the war—the way the story is told—is a pure reflection of the attitude of the British right after the war toward the Indians, who were promised countless concessions for their unnerving support in aiding the Allied Forces.

The Congress expected some form of discourse over the idea of separation and their dominion; they believed that the unsettled focus of the Crown due to the war at hand would benefit their cause.

The Muslim League expected some input toward their goal of independence as well. Alas, all concessions offered were remnants of previous ones, and they went in vain.

The subjects' anger was also aggravated by the fact that their consent had not been taken in the first place—they were just expected to bear the burden of Britain.

Thus, the rivalry between the colonizers and their subjects, and the rivalries between the subjects themselves, had boiled up to the point that the 1940s looked like the climax of the past two hundred years of colonial rule.

Many people feared the Indians were on the brink of a civil war. Gandhi had reverted to *Satyagarah*, and, this time, it was on a much larger scale as civil disobedience pertained under the name of the "Quit India Movement."

The demand had become more urgent—Congress wanted immediate withdrawal of the British, with control being handed over to a Constituent Assembly (basically under Congress' power).

The Muslim League was naturally angered at this proposal because, to them, it aimed to antagonize the British and solidified the fact that Congress wanted a Hindu dominion rather than shared control.

However, some hope emerged on the brink of the horizon in the form of a letter. It was intended for Mr. Jinnah and was sent by Mahatma Gandhi himself.

The letter sparked what became known as the Gandhi-Jinnah talks of 1944. The two leaders of the opposing factions sat down, face to face, at Jinnah's residence in Bombay.

Gandhi's intention for this meeting was to convince Jinnah of the absurdity of the idea of Pakistan. However, Jinnah maintained that he saw no future in which the two groups co-exist in a harmonious sphere.

He concluded that the Lahore Resolution would remain the league's official policy. And so, the light at the horizon's end disappeared as the talks broke off.

However, the British were determined to make dying efforts to re-establish control or influence over the people they had colonized for a long time.

Under such circumstances, Lord Wavell, the viceroy of India at the time, after a detailed discussion with the British Crown, invited all major political parties of India to a conference at Shimla in 1945.

There he proposed the idea of a Viceroy's executive council to make administrative decisions. For the first time, the British wanted nominees to represent different groups of India in this council.

But one can argue that this proposition was made far too late as the talks failed when the Muslim League and Congress started arguing about the party which truly represented the Muslims of India.

The Congress had sent Maulana Azad as a Muslim representative to claim that Congress also represented Muslim rights. The Muslim League, on the other hand, had a different opinion.

Chaos had ensued throughout India owing to the results of the general elections of 1946. The Muslims complained of unfair and illicit treatment at the hands of the Hindus, and non-cooperation between India's two major political parties made the British government fearful of a political deadlock. Hence the Cabinet Mission Plan was sent in 1946 under the watchful eye of Lord Lawrence.

The Cabinet boiled down to establishing a union of India, divided into an Executive and a Legislature.

The residuary power would go to the provinces, and an interim government would be set up if it supported the Congress and the Muslim League. This chaos was followed by confusion. The Muslim League agreed to these demands, and while the Congress had previously agreed, it afterward rejected the idea of an interim government.

Seeing this, the Muslim League, too, decided to back off from the Cabinet Mission Plan and its proposals, and they declared a "Direct Action" day.

This was a demonstration at the hands of the Muslim League to display their power and solidify the demand for a separate nation.

However, the rallies soon turned ugly, and it was reported that in Calcutta, at Jallianwala Bagh, it turned into a massive riot that claimed the lives of around 4000 people, thus leaving a blood-smeared mark at the back of the League.

At this point, the new Viceroy, Lord Mountbatten, had become convinced that there was no further point in discussing with the Indians, nor was it sensible to hope for any collaboration between the Hindus and Muslims.

It had become clear to them that the immediate path of action would be to devise a plan regarding the transfer of control between the two superpowers of the Indian state in a responsible manner.

Thus, the June 3rd plan was born, and the British government approved it. However, it is alleged that the program was disapproved and altered by Nehru, who was staying at Lord Mountbatten's residence in India.

He got Mountbatten to draft another one more suited to his needs and approve it again. Therefore, the conflict over the division of resources between the Hindus and the Muslims began.

This conflict seeped into every possible resource concerning the two states. The so-called Radcliffe Award, which was responsible for drawing a boundary between the two states, was heavily criticized by the Muslim League.

They had reservations over the division of states that include, but are not limited to, Bharatpur, Alwar, Chittagong, and Assam, as they alleged that these were Muslim-majority states that rightfully belonged to their country.

Conflict arose over the division of water resources and was only cleared (to some extent) years later in the form of the Indus Water Treaty. They even alleged that the military assets awarded to the Muslims were old and worn out.

However, the largest issue of concern, which is still a major cause of disagreement between the two states, arrived over Kashmir.

Given its geographical topology and strategic location on the world map, Jammu and Kashmir presented an exceptional economic opportunity that was coveted by both nations owing to its distinct advantages. This ensured a territorial conflict over Kashmir that is present to this day. Even now, Jammu and Kashmir are disputed territories divided between the borders of the two states.

Regardless of the tumult, India and Pakistan were born. India was officially given the birth date of 15th August 1947. However, things were not as simple as the two countries now faced a massive refugee crisis as citizens who wanted to shift to the opposite states found themselves in the wrong land.

Thus started a massive migration on both sides that resulted in a huge amount of blood loss as riots broke down in the pathway to the two states on either side. This marked the tragic birth of the two nations.

Jawaharlal Nehru, the pioneer of the Indian National Congress, took office on 15th August 1947, and it can be reasonably argued that he ensured that India did the best it could manage as a new country.

Just two years later, he was able to draft and present a constitution for the government, officially replacing the Government of India Act of 1935.

He stood his ground as Pakistani forces tried to take control of the regal state of Kashmir and led India through the first Indo-Pak war of 1947-48.

From defending the country from further future threats from Pakistan to urbanization to increasing the rights and self-determination of women, the Nehru administration won future elections decisively and provided India the ground it needed to turn into the grand hub of industrialization and modernity it is today. India managed to do all that while making sure that its diverse set of cultural values remained intact.

Since we now have a hefty idea of the history, we will investigate my travels as I take you through the diversity that I mentioned above in the accounts of my travels throughout the different states of India. Stick through this journey with me!

CHAPTER 9:

TAJ MAHAL

To truly understand India and get familiar with the plethora of blooming cultures, practices, and people here, one needs to delve into its history. History offers insight and context into the brilliant spectacles of this nation.

Despite the technological advances that India has now become home to, it still is, by nature, a historical and mystical place. It is this history that lives through its roots and presents an image of India today—modern India.

As we point towards the North, we witness this history as much as we witness the nation's modernity. One can say that its modernity exists only because of the place's historical significance.

To the North, we gaze at the heart of this beautiful and culturally-rich nation, and like an actual heart, we see the diversity being combined and pumped out to the rest of the country. Delhi truly operates as the central organ of India.

In a political context, it might be one of the most important cities in India because Delhi runs the bureaucratic machinery of the nation. It has the title of the country's capital, and being a commercial, transport, and cultural hub, it truly lives up to that name.

Delhi itself is a division between the New and the Old. As you walk through the mellow streets of Old Delhi, you'll find some spiritual resonance, regardless of where you are from. This is perhaps because of the city sitting, like an ancient resort, astride the torrents of the Yamuna River.

As a tributary of the Great Ganges, Yamuna flows, purifying the very vessel of this city and, with it, the hearts of those who dwell in it. The tides of this river carry the weight of the swarm of civilizations that have been through this area that is now Uttar Pradesh.

This weight can be felt in the spirit of a true traveler as they gaze across the wide banks of it while crossing the ancient Yamuna Bridge. The very bridge itself is a spectacle of the past. Beneath the modern clusters of steel rails and cement, its foundations carry the memory of its roots that age back to the 17th century, when it was first constructed.

Within this old district stands a stunning depiction of human architecture. The tall, red sandstone walls of this building give it its name—the Red Fort or *"Lal Qila."* The monument stands as a relic of the past, as the history of this region is as old as the still-standing walls of the fort.

Built by the famous Shah Jehan in 1648, the monument truly boasts the peak of Mughal design. One can walk through the famous Lahore Gate, so named as it faces Lahore in Pakistan. Or they can enter through the even grander Delhi Gate, an entrance once used by the emperor for his spectacular processions.

The Lahore Gate is synonymous in its nature with a real-life time machine as walking through it, one enters the Chatta Chowk and is instantly transported to the past. You find yourself in a place like a 17th century market during the reign of Shah Jehan.

Strolling through this place, with the vendors screaming at the top of their lungs, the hustle and bustle of the crowds, and the stalls displaying items of gold, gems, and silk, is no less than watching an old movie starring yourself.

But if you find yourself in search of an even older heritage—perhaps the Muslim roots of this region—you can climb the tallest minaret and look at the breathtaking view of the city in 360 degrees and peer down at the Qutub Minar below you—yet another ancient mural that Delhi has to offer.

This ornately-crafted, five-story tower rises to 70 meters and offers a display gleaming with intricate carvings, inscriptions from the Quran (the Holy Book of Islam), and architectural prowess as each story was constructed with a different type of stone. It is now also a UNESCO World Heritage site.

Delhi, by large, is home to many other forts and monuments ranging from the Old Qila (old fort) to the Gurudwara Bangla Sahib, all of which guard their ancient secrets. But the city has more to offer if you search for something more modern.

The sacred Yamuna flows as a natural divide between the city's two parts, and what you are looking for lays across the other side—welcome to New Delhi. Perhaps the most enticing thing to do, even for the locals here, is to wait for the dark of the night to see the India Gate lit up in an aurora borealis of colors. The gate honors the lives of the Indian soldiers who died in the Second World War.

The symbolic heart located in Old Delhi flows gently into the booming metropolis that is New Delhi. The modern mixes with the culture here, creating a peculiar blend. One can witness this in the view of the Lotus Temple, the bustling malls, government buildings, art tours, and the kitchens and restaurants offering a mix of local and continental cuisine.

But there is much more to Northern India than the capital. It can be said that if one truly wishes to flip the history book of India, then the right place to visit is the city of Agra. One only needs to follow the ancient path of the holy Yamuna downstream from Delhi to reach the historical paradise of Agra.

When travelers picture India, they often bring the Mughal image into their minds. Agra transcends above that as the city is believed to be founded during the Muslim Sultanate era before Babur took control of it after the first Battle of Panipat in 1526.

This city features an incredible white-stone masterpiece and a World Heritage site known to the world as the Taj Mahal.

However, as you walk through the gates of this monument to catch the early morning sun glistening against its white peak in a fluorescence of yellow and orange hue, you walk alongside the calm water canals flowing alongside the ornamentally crafted gardens. As you appreciate the handwork masterpiece of 20,000 laborers in the floral carvings on the white marble, remind yourself of the lesser-known tragic history of this place.

The Taj Mahal is not a reflection of architecture but of everlasting love. The monument was built in emperor Shah Jehan's mourning for his late wife, Mumtaz Mahal, to pay tribute to her as she passed away during childbirth. The veins of their eternal love flow through every brick and every inch of this building to this day.

But if you seem tired of the immense crowd gathered around and inside the Mahal and are searching for some much-needed serenity, do not leave the city just yet. Follow the trail of the Yamuna through the Mahal and find solace at the Mehtab Bagh—the Moonlight Garden.

With its eye-catching scenery and gleaming flowers, this garden complex is a remarkable sight in the moonlight or as the sun sets across the horizon. Come here if you are in a desperate search for peace and spiritual awakening, and witness the tranquil garden connect you closer to nature and everything else that matters. The good news is that this is just one of the therapeutic parks that the Mughals left in this city.

A marble may be the one stone that is associated with Agra and truly represents its history. If you have a soft spot for ornately crafted stone pieces and wish to take some of them home, head to the Subash Emporium and dive deep into the breathtaking display of stone handiwork. From floral pots to China pieces to souvenirs, this place has everything to satisfy your love for this kind of mastery.

If you truly wish for Agra to surround you and grasp your vision immediately, visit the famous Fatehpur Sikri, where you will be surrounded by the beauty of Akbar's architectural investments. Fatehpur Sikri was once the empire's capital, and Akbar referred to it as the City of Victory—a tribute to his military conquests.

Tourists often pay tribute to Sufi Shaikh Salim Chishti, just like Akbar, as they walk through the magnificent Jama Masjid courtyards. Not only is this a heritage site, but it is also an actively-used mosque for the congregational prayers of Muslims.

If the bright white marble is getting too much for your taste palette, Agra still has much more to offer you. Walk through the vast, centuries-old, red sandstone castles located at the Agra fort or take a stroll at the Indo-Persian-styled *Chini ka Rauza*, one of the few structures in India to feature the under-rated craftsmanship of Chini—tiles made from yellow and green glazed turquoise.

The capital city of the Rajasthan state of India offers a final blow to your traveling tastebuds. Often referred to as the Paris of India and the Island of Glory, the ancient city of Jaipur can be categorized as a heritage site. The city beholds some of the most intricate and unique displays of architecture that distinguish it from the rest of India.

The best way to sum up the unique style of Jaipur, one should visit the Hawa Mahal. It is hard not to stare at the beauty of this place for hours. The front veranda of the building is populated with rows of tiny salmon-pink windows and geometric accents. It has around 953 windows making it an airy and breezy summer destination. The honeycomb-like façade of the monument is a tribute to the Hindu god Krishna's crown and makes it a remarkable sight as it justly captures the glory of the God it refers to.

CHAPTER 10:

THE JEWEL OF KANPUR

Regarding the North, India seems to have increasingly more to show. Whether the land's simple and serene natural beauty or the intermingling of different cultures, it has everything to soothe the taste of a traveling palette. In the spirit of this discussion, it would be fitting to say that one necessary place to visit in India on your list should be Kanpur.

The city stands some 80 kilometers away from the banks of the Great River Ganga, and the mystical water runs deep within the soil of this town as it carries this city which is now regarded as the industrial hub of Uttar Pradesh, holds the weight of great history—one marked with blood and tragedy, but also beauty.

There is some debate about the city's origin, but whichever history book we read, we will find some commonality in the importance of this place due to its location—the proximity of the Ganga blesses this piece of Earth. Some argue that King Hindu Singh founded the city.

Others believe the city is associated with the Karna of the Mahabharata period. Its industrial importance, especially in the context of its geography, was recognized by the British, who established garrisons here after defeating the Nawab of Awadh.

But the British arrival was ill-fated, too, because when history unfolded, it left this city with blood stains that would forever mark the waters flowing alongside it. In 1857, one of the major events that marked an end to the Indian War of Independence was the Kanpur Massacre. As the British troops laid siege to the city, they offered a way out to the rebels in return for their leader, Nana Sahib. Their procession out of the city became a huge bloodbath as most men were killed.

However, the city has not let the city define itself because it has come a long way from the events of 1857. In fact, Kanpur has been called the Manchester of India in recent years. The reason for this perhaps lies in that, unlike other old cities of India, Kanpur has a sleek blend of the modern and the historical now embedded within its structure, making it the best of both worlds.

The modern comes in a wave with places like the Blue World theme park, which is a water park based on multiple aesthetics and themes such as Mayan, Egyptian, European, and Indian. But it also comes in the form of high rises and lavish brands like those in *Khazana Market*, known for hosting high-end apparel in garments, leather, perfumes, and jewelry. Then there is also the industrial suburb famous for its leather production called *Jajmau*.

On the other hand, the historical sits still, perfectly harmonious with the new. This is evident in the serenity offered by the lush green sites of Nana Sahib Park and Mahatma Gandhi Park. Both are ancient gardens built to honor two respected names of Indian history, and both live up to that image. But while the narrative may be more abstract here, it becomes clearer at the Kanpur museum, where there is an array of displays of artifacts and paintings from the colonial period.

But the striking part about Kanpur is that most places here do not truly belong to the modern or historical period. Most of them exist as a blend between the two, and the common factor among them is that they are usually built in honor of a deity that Hindus hold dear. We can take the example of the curious façade of the *"Kanch ka Mandir"* or the

Glass Temple here. This place of worship, adorned with colorful pieces of glass, was built to honor the Lord Mahavira.

Then we have the Mughal-inspired architectural phenomenon of the ISKCON temple, an International spiritual tourist attraction. The white marble and high-rising domes are dedicated to Lord Krishna. But perhaps the one place that is as ancient in its location as its practices and has been intact during this modernization is the Brahmavart Ghat. This is also a good place to begin our discussion regarding the unique cultural traditions of Kanpur.

The Brahmavart Ghat is considered the holiest of all the ghats (diving or submerging points) in India and is dedicated to the Hindu God, Brahma. The devotees come from all over India to indulge in a curious practice that has lasted centuries. They take a ritual bath in the Holy Ganga and then gather at the Wooden Slipper's altar to offer their prayers and show obedience and submission to the deity.

The best way to discuss the unique cultural blend that reflects and represents the city is by visiting the fairs here. The best one to look out for is called the annual Ganga Fair. It is held just five days after the annual *Holi* celebration of Hindus, and the festival is marked by visitors getting a taste of the local culture. The artistic element of the city is truly reflected here through various events such as dance practices and poem recitation. It is a cultural night.

But this element of intermingling is not just unique to Kanpur. As we move toward the southern part of Uttar Pradesh, still staying close to the roots of the Ganga, we might find ourselves lucky enough to stumble upon the Kumbh Mela at Allahabad, a celebration that happens every 12 years. It takes place at one of the most significant locations of the city, if not the entire country, the Triveni Sangam.

The point is special because it uniquely lies at a position where the Holy River Ganges, the Yamuna, and the mythical River of Sarasvati meet. This religious gathering is known to have more than 30 million attendees each time, and they all cleanse their souls as they bathe in the waters of Ganga, asking for salvation. But Allahabad is more than just about ritualistic gatherings around its Holy Rivers. It is known for its colorful traditions.

Apart from being populated with mandirs, each having an architectural structure as equally beautiful as the other, the city of Allahabad is also known to be a bustling metropolis. Nostalgia and tradition are filled to the brim in the tall glasses of Lassi at Raja Ram's. The chaat at Nirala is enough to make your mouth water just by looking at it. Hira Halwai's gulab jamuns melt in your mouth, and the age-old, infamous kachori and sabzi at Netram Mulchand and Sons is something to die for. Allahabad screams values, traditions, and culture, and the authenticity of its street food validates this.

But the presence of all of this is not entirely ubiquitous to the entirety of the Northern Sector of India. Toward the North-Western side of Uttar Pradesh lies the inhospitable Thar Desert, located within the territory of Rajasthan. It is known to be the largest state of India and home to some of the country's most important cities, such as Jaipur and Udaipur. The city's name translates to an exciting interpretation, "The Abode of the Rajas (kings)."

But outside these cities, the Thar desert makes life extremely difficult and harsh with its extreme climate as shrub vegetation. The weather can vary from extremely arid to humid, making predictability harder. But despite the tough conditions, you will find the cities populated with a blend of people. The Jats, Gujars, and Brahmans belong to all sorts of modes of belief. Because of the desert, you will find that a major chunk of the population in this state, living close to or in the desert, belongs to Bedouin tribes that practice a migratory lifestyle.

In conclusion, the Northern states of India are special because they all have something different to offer. On paper, it seems that the cultural blend in these places and the general lifestyle takes a lot from the historical context of it but adds a modern touch to it. No part overpowers the other. They exist in perfect harmony to complement each other. They create a truly spectacular and curious image of the great Northern regions of India.

CHAPTER 11:

GOLDEN TEMPLE

We are still following the flow of the Great Ganga, but this time, we are flowing with a slight tendency toward the West as we follow the northern route from New Delhi. Here we come across a lush green land between River Ganges on the East and River Hindon on the West. Welcome to the fertile plains of Meerut.

When I think of Meerut, or anyone thinks of Meerut, they imagine rich plains with deposits of alluvium and a flourished agricultural setting. While all that is true, and we will talk about it, Meerut is also much more than that.

The first thing it is known for is its blessed climate, despite India being an equatorial region. The summer months can have temperatures as high as 45 degrees Celsius, while the winters can go as low as 2 degrees Celsius. In that sense, it matches the taste of different kinds of people.

Monsoon lightly brushes this region throughout the end of June and lasts till the end of September, and, in this way, the region is nourished with all the natural rainwater it needs to fulfill the needs of its agricultural production. In these months, the Ganges and Yamuna bring blessings through their tributaries as heaps of fertile alluvium are deposited on the banks, making it ideal for plantations.

This aids in the prosperity this region has achieved in the agricultural sector. The area is known to grow food and cash crops that include, but are not limited to wheat, bajra, maize, and barley. Sugar industries have sprouted throughout the plains, making it an extremely lucrative business, and so have dairy products-based industries and agro-based manufacture. This makes the region well-equipped to be called an industrial giant as well.

But there is a huge diversity in how industries have spread across the region. The part has switched to manufacturing and producing sports, musical, and surgical goods in the past decade. But, as I said, it is more than just agriculture and industries. Meerut is a boiling pot of different cultures that have existed since before the birth of Christ.

In the current climate, the population is mainly dominated by Rajput, Tyagis, Jats, and the Gujjar community. Each of these groups adds to the mix of cultural heritage in this region, and it is evident in the architectural structure of this place and the vibrant fairs and festivals that sprout here throughout the year.

One of the most famous celebrations home to this region is the Nauchandi Fair, a thirty-day-long fair held after the first week of Holi. This celebration has survived nearly 350 years, solidifying it into a significant local tradition. Throughout the 30 days, renowned musicians from all over the country arrive and display their talents. Thousands of stall line the market areas with a rich display of aircraft and handiwork such as pottery and ceramics. Furthermore, new additions such as beauty pageants have intermingled into this age-old practice.

Sports, in recent years, has grown to an immense scale here as Meerut is now regarded as one of the "sports cities of India" due to the thriving sports goods manufacturing industry here. *Kabadi*—wrestling—is also popularly practiced here.

There is an invigorating spiritual and mystical element to this place that has been here for centuries, and it has taken shape in the very movement and fluidity of the physical bodies living here. By this, I am referring to the dances such as Kathak, among other folk dances, that are said to have originated here. Participating in music and cultural dance practices is considered necessary among all generations.

While Meerut may not be considered a central city of India, it would not be bold, by any measure, to say that it is the historic central city of this region. Because as mentioned a few chapters before, we know it all started from Meerut. The birth of nationalism in South Asia took a spark from this place.

The revolt of 1857 took birth from this place due to the execution of Mangal Pandey, and that gave strength to a national spirit among Indians and sowed seeds for the demand for a separate state later. Meerut was the birthplace of this spirit that eventually formed India (and Pakistan).

The historical events and the mixed culture carried throughout the centuries have amalgamated into a serenity offered by this place's beautiful manufactured architectural elements. One such feature can be seen at the Jain Mandir Salawa, located in the very heart of the village of Salawa.

Here one can witness the beauty of the hand-crafted sculptures of different Hindu deities. The temple itself is associated with Lord Rishabhdeva, whose sculptures are ornated in gold and black marble here, offering spiritual reconciliation and anthropological relevance to this place.

However, if you are searching for peace, a special kind that can only be found in the turbulent events of the past, the perfect place to visit would be the Shahid Smarak Park of Meerut. This place has vivid sculptural displays of the Revolt of 1857, standing in no order and surrounded by the serene climate of the park. One cannot help but feel calm here, knowing that they are sitting in a place that came into existence thanks to the sacrifices of their ancestors.

However, if one was to zoom out from the lens of the world and take a precise look at North Western India, Meerut is not the first place that would come into their sight. Their vision would be impaired by a gleaming golden light shining from the roof of a dome ornated and decorated in gold. They would find themselves staring at the great city of Amritsar. More specifically, they would witness the cultural, historical, and physical might of the Golden Temple of Amritsar.

The Golden Temple is a budding spot for old and new Sikh pilgrims because it is marked with sacredness and sanctity for them. While the mandir is built entirely out of marble, the golden dome is completely covered with gold bricks constructed by Maharaja Ranjit Singh, who commissioned it to be covered with almost 400 kg of gold plates.

The crowded temple is visited daily by pilgrims with covered heads who offer sacrifices and pray intently. The reason they associate such spiritual importance to this mandir is that it is said that the Sage Valmiki, who wrote the spic Ramayana, Sita, and Rama, spent his 14-year exile in Amritsar leaving a mark of metaphysical significance on the city. This is carried by the monks here who regularly offer free food to almost 20,000 people here daily as they offer their visits.

Once we have absorbed the light of this great temple, we can proceed slightly south while still maintaining our overall North-Western incline, and we will reach the city of Ludhiana. This city once stood on the banks of the Sutlej River, but it is 8 miles south of its present course. Much like Meerut, the city is home to an immense agricultural output. The areas surrounding the region are richly cultivated with plantations, including wheat, corn, cotton, and peanuts.

This city is extremely agriculturally and industrially because it is located right between the grand trunk road that passes through it along with several rail lines, making it well-connected to the entire country. The height of its agricultural importance is such that the famous Punjab University of Agriculture, teaching the sciences behind the profession, is located there.

There is a diverse mix of the Hindu and Sikh populations there that are known to live in harmony, and that is evident in the multitudes of cultural practices and festivals that people partake in here. Ludhiana is said to be a land of colorful fairs and events, and it truly lives up to that name. Unsurprisingly, many of these festivals revolve around their agricultural importance too.

One such example is the Lohri festival, celebrated on the last day of Poh, and the Baisakhi, their annual harvest festival commemorating the hardship of the farmers working to their fullest extent the entire year. It includes fanfare, fireworks, and huge celebrations—things that the people of Ludhiana remember and look forward to the whole of the year.

CHAPTER 12:

THE GREAT CORNERS OF CHENNAI

The Great Ganges will continue its flow for hundreds of years, but if we deviate slightly from its course, we will notice that there is more to see in the great nation of India than just the cities that follow the course of the river. We will now take a deeper diver towards India's Southern and South Eastern regions.

As we enter the Tamil Nadu state of India and reach its southeastern coast, we will find ourselves in a land located on the flat coastal plains of the Bay of Bengal, and the locals call this place the gateway to South India—it only gets more vibrant after this. Welcome to the great city of Chennai.

The great history of India has a lot of association with the rivers that flow through it. Some even say that these rivers are a very symbolic representation of the flow of this history. Chennai is no exception to this rule either, as we unfold the rich history of this region by reading the waters flowing through it.

Chennai was originally referred to as Madras Patnam and was located between the Pennar River of Nellore and the Pennar River of Cuddalore. The city existed way before the Mughal era and colonization and has seen the rule of many different families.

The Chola family originally ruled over it in the 2nd century AD, and a century later, it saw a shift in control to their rivals, the Pallavas. After a series of back-and-forth battles, the authority again shifted to the Cholas, and eventually, the Chola supremacy ended when the Pandya family defeated them.

The rule of Pandyas lasted for over half a century when the Bahimini Kingdom took over as part of the Delhi Sultanate. In this way, the region (larger than the city we know today) saw continuous shifts in control for over 5 centuries until it eventually came under the power of the Mughal Empire in 1687 with the fall of Golkonda.

Such is the dynamics of this power shift that Chennai even briefly went under French control in 1744, only to be restored under English control in 1749 through a peace accord. In the 18th century, the British also saw the usefulness of Chennai's geographical location owing to its proximity to the Bay of Bengal and decided to establish it as a Naval Base, which it still is today.

If we fast forward to the present time and peer at Chennai from a zoomed-out lens, we can see why it had been a historically important place to reside in. Currently, Chennai is the fourth-largest metropolis of India with its boom of highrises, businesses, street-food sites, universities, and many more local attractions.

One obviously cannot go to Chennai and not visit the splendid beaches here. Marina Beach is the longest natural urban beach in the country, the world's eleventh longest, and Besant Nagar Beach is an extended part of the 2nd longest beach in the World.

The interesting thing about this region is that it is a perfect blend between the modern and the historical, coming together in a blissful façade. The city hosts unique, modern attractions such as the VGP Snow

Kingdom, a full-fledged snow theme park, while also being home to the architectural splendor of the ancient cultural roots of Hinduism in the form of the Kapaleeshwarar Temple.

Being a bustling metropolis, it is only natural that diversity can be expected from this region. While Tamil is the main official language of the region, you will find people here speaking everything from English, Urdu, Telugu, and Punjabi.

This diversity will be evident in the food, and the taste here has no substitute all over the country. This can be said about South India because this part of the country hosts cuisines that are amazingly different from the rest of the country, and Chennai is a good entry spot for these delicacies.

The streets offer dishes such as sambhar, uttapam, dosa, vadas, idlis, mendu, and many other dishes that have been perfected and passed on over the centuries. People from all over the country flood the streets of places like Richie Street, Mount Road, Burma Bazaar, and Anna Nagar for their famous lines of street food vendors.

Push carts, sidewalk vendors, and food trucks all add to the bustle of these places as different aromas inundate the air. Among the most famous street food here is the Atho Man, originally a Burmese dish, but people have forgotten about that due to its popularity in Chennai.

This is a burst of different flavors on a plate, including a bed of colored noodles mixed with fresh vegetables and an array of sauces. Then there is also the never-ending love people have here for the century-old paani puris. You might even be in an intense argument on the streets with a stranger regarding the best Paani Puri place in Chennai.

The soft, crunchy coating of these delicious balls filled with potato, imli chutney, ragda, and green chutney is brought together in spicy, tangy water that bursts into your mouth as you take a bite of this pocket-sized delight. Then there is also Chennai's very own Podi disa, a delicious and spicy dosa soaked in red podi that will severely battle your spice tolerance but leave you asking for more.

But if we really must talk about street food, we cannot forget about the nook and cranny of each person walking the streets of Chennai, the cornerstone of the street food staple: Vada—the deep friend donut made from spices and gram, served with coconut chutney or sambhar.

Practice and display of arts are precious assets in society here. Chennai was once known for organizing the Chennai Sangamam in January every year, displaying different forms of arts practiced in Tamil Nadu here. The same goes for music, as an entire 5-day festival is dedicated to it by the Madras Music Academy.

However, if we divert a little further away from Chennai and move further South, following the course of the Deccan Plateau, and take a swift turn into the tributary of Krishna River called the Musi River, we will soon find ourselves in a lower-central region of India that beholds wonders. We now stand in the old city of Hyderabad.

Much like Chennai, the culture of Hyderabad finds itself in a unique position since it is a blend of the modern and traditional; it seems to have taken qualities that make it the best of both worlds. However, the district's origins have been traced back to the Mauryan civilization.

However, the city was officially founded and became what we know today in the 1500s under the Qutb Shah dynasty, which explains why many people and cultures still inhabit it. However, despite its modern transition, you will find remnants of the Qutb Shah dynasty throughout the city.

The first and brightest example is the high-reaching Golconda Fort, located a few kilometers outside the main city. This extraordinary architectural masterpiece consists of 8 gates and 87 bastions with majestic walls that rise as high as 18 feet.

Such a blend of people coexisting within the same city is only perceivable if there is some sense of equanimity among the community, and this becomes clear through the great statue of Equality adorned in gold that stands in this city. This Hindu god statue, Sri Ramanujacharya Swamy, is decorated in gold and requires a steep climb of 108 steps to reach it. It is believed that the long-reaching eye of the statue showers blessings upon the city as it has over the years.

But, if you have come to Hyderabad not for the sights but after hearing stories of ornaments, stones, gold, silk, and ornately-sown clothes, then head right to the Laad Bazaar. You will find yourself surrounded by the hustle and bustle of vendors and hawkers selling an incomparable variety of bangles, pearls, and other jewelry.

Being a social and cultural junction, the city naturally gives back to the state in a lot of different ways when it comes to the economy because the natural diversity of the city is also evident in its role in India's economy.

The industries here range from retail and real estate to high-rising Information Technology firms, which are further given a boost in their cause through the fast-flowing tourism industry here.

The enticing thing about this city, however, is that it has a strange sense of comfort—the ability to make itself the home of anyone. Over here, no one is a stranger, and it is often the little things here that you will find yourself staying for. You will come for the jewelry and find yourself staying for the kite festivals. Such is the simple charm of the city.

As we continue, we will dive deeper into the South Indian states of India and how the difference between the Northern and Southern regions of India is a divide that casts nothing but beauty on the country's silhouette.

South Indians, as we will see, are a staple of the country known for their versatility. This is evident in how the emergence of IT technology in places like Chennai and Gujrat has led to South Indians taking great leaps in these sectors. This is also evident in how 80% of all H-1B Immigrant Visas in the USA are occupied by Indians, mostly from areas like Chennai and Gujrat.

CHAPTER 13:

GREAT SPICES

Let's pause the Southern flow of the Ganges. In fact, let us break the river's flow altogether and urge the Gods gently sway the water to reverse the tide. Let us take the course of the river in the opposite direction. Are you here with me? Can you feel the clock of time ticking backward? Now imagine yourself in pre-18th-century Europe.

The Age of Exploration began in Europe, where they had ships docking on the great plains of the Americas. But people like Vasco da Gama yearned to discover the mystical lands of the subcontinent—the area we now call India. The main reason for this was not just the mystery of it all but also because they had already had a taste of the lands (quite literally) through the means of Muslim traders in the areas of Spain.

The Europeans had become addicted to the spices coming in from the lands belonging to the subcontinent, and they wanted to break into the profitable trading prospects. The Dutch, French, and English all had the same intention. Such was the grab of these mystical spices that we have grown so familiar with and often take for granted. It would not even be crude to say that any history of the subcontinent is bound to be incomplete without a mention of the famous spices originating in these lands.

These are locally called "masala," and the familiar taste, scent, and consistency of Indian foods are not the same without them. These include ginger, turmeric, fenugreek, cumin, cardamom, cilantro, and the famous garam masala. India was naturally a place that the Europeans were attracted to when it came to breaking into the spice trade because of the physical attributes of the lands.

The place was, and is, perfect for growing spices. Turmeric, coriander, and black pepper require ideal climatic conditions, such as high rainfall and humidity. Being close to the equator, India provided all this effortlessly, making it a lucrative spice breeding ground. Such was the attraction of this trade that it fueled as a source of motivation for entire expeditions to India.

Now open your eyes and return to the river. You now understand how important and deep the roots of these delicacies are in India. So let us now explore what the contemporary state of spices is here. And what other place to go except the great state of Karnataka? Here our first stop is its capital and largest city, the age-old city of Bangalore.

This large-scale commercial and residential city of India started once as a mere mud fort built by Emperor Kempe Gowda in 1537. It was later expanded by Kempe Gowda's son, who also worked on its beautification. Eventually, it came under British colonial rule, where it served as British administrative headquarters, and they maintained a high administrative and military presence there.

The original name of the city is said to be Bangavaluru, and there is a famed tale associated with this name. It is said that King Veera Ballala of the Hoysala Dynasty once traveled through the jungle surrounding the place, and the journey was extremely hard for the traveling party. It came to a point where they had nothing left to eat, and they came across an elderly, impoverished woman who had nothing to offer them except boiled beans. The monarch was so overjoyed with pleasure that he named the whole city "Benda Kaal Ooru," which roughly translates to "city of boiling beans."

Apart from its rich history, Bangalore has become a popular tourist destination in the past few decades because of how rich the city is both in terms of its modern facilities and ancient roots. If you ask any local, you are guaranteed to be suggested to visit the beloved Church Street at least once in your stay here. It is one of the city's busiest streets, home to gift shops, music stores, bookstores, cafes, and of course, the main attraction, the Cathedral. Despite the name, people from different religions intermingle seamlessly and beautifully on this long strip of road.

But if you are not one for crowds, then there is always the sanctity offered by the Lalbagh botanical gardens. This bonsai, topiary, lotus, and rose garden uses modern technology to preserve nature. But most importantly, the serenity it offers when you sit at the bank of the indoor lake is other-worldly.

Perhaps you want to enjoy a peaceful and lively picnic surrounded by Mother Earth. But you do not just want to go to any park. You want to go somewhere that is rich in cultural heritage. You want to be surrounded by art and history. Look no further and take the first cab to the famous Bangalore palace, a royal fort with beautiful grounds surrounded by picturesque architecture that one can admire all day.

But as I said, the best part about a walk in this city is that you will immerse yourself in both the old and the modern. Take a short tour of the Innovative Film City, a local attraction, which is an Indian movie theme park where you will find rides, museums, and adventure sports. Want something more challenging and heart-throbbing? Race to the Wonderla Amusement Park, where you may find yourself screaming at the top of your lungs as the rollercoaster drives you into the air at gut-wrenching speeds.

But perhaps by this point, you are tired of the bounds of a city. You want some more freedom, some more thrill. Well, Karnataka has more to offer. As you proceed towards the state's Western side, you will reach the sister or twin city of Bangalore, located on the West Coast of India, bordered by the Arabian Sea and the Western Ghats: welcome to Mangalore!

While Bangalore's focus had mostly been on architecture are heritage, Mangalore brings you to the wilds as you will find long stretches of beaches and golf courses here. This also makes it a popular tourist resort, just like its twin. The brown sands contrast with the serene blue of the salty sea, accompanied by coral reefs, clams, crabs, and mangroves, as you take a trip across Ullai Beach and Panambur Beach. Panambur Beach is a "must-visit" destination because the locals have commodified it into a mini resort.

But know that Mangalore has a lot to show off regarding architecture, too. You need to know where to look. Or, in this case, where to look from because I am talking about the breathtaking structure that stands on top of Lighthouse Hill in the form of St. Aloysius Chapel—a regal and elegant depiction of human architectural strength.

Now, let's go back to where we started. The reason I started this chapter with a journey into the spice culture of India was to enunciate the importance that Karnataka holds in this regard. The entire region is booming and bustling with the production and sale of local spices that are popular throughout the country and the world. Just take the example of the Red gram native to Kalaburagi. This type of daal is grown in around 70% of the agricultural land in the district. It is known for its superior taste and aroma but also for taking relatively less time to cook.

The brilliant shades of the fresh and dry figs of Ballari are another popular local demand that has seen an immense boost in popularity in recent years. Apart from being a good energy source, they also have medicinal importance. The Kodagu district is home to some of the finest grade Arabica and Robusta coffee beans all over Karnataka that are known to have a distinct chocolaty flavor and aroma. And let's not forget the robust red of the Byadgi chilies grown in the Haveri district, which are a staple in every Indian kitchen—house or restaurant.

From modernity to ancient architecture to an array of spices, Karnataka State has everything that one would want. It could perhaps be regarded as one of the most versatile states of India in terms of its socioeconomic structure, tourist attractions, and residential and commercial outputs.

CHAPTER 14:

TOLLYWOOD

The South of India still has a lot more to show, and this chapter will focus on exactly that but also in quite literal terms as we will dive deep into the show-biz industry of India. As we discussed earlier, these Southern cities are a bloom of diversity in terms of their people, culture, religion, and societal organization.

As we approach the banks of the Bay of Bengal, the tide seems ever flowing, ever replacing, but it carries the weight of the immense history that populated these very shores. Standing on the edge of this Bay is the city of Visakhapatnam.

Like numerous other cities in India, Visakhapatnam thrives with deep-seated roots of history and culture that stretch back centuries. The city derived its name from Visakha, the Hindu deity associated with bravery and warfare.

According to the local legend, the city was named Visakhapatnam by a king between the 9th and 11th centuries. The local story states that the king was so captivated by the beauty of this place that he decided to build a temple there in honor of his family deity, Visakha.

And much like other cities throughout India, it had been ruled by several dynasties over the years. These include the Kalingas, the Chankyas, the Rajahmundry kings, and the famous Cholas.

Such was the diverse change in control that, by the end of the 18th century, the city came under French rule and eventually got transferred to the British. One could argue that the city's true commercial popularity commenced after this point.

The British East India Company established trading operations here and a factory which started the industrial boom. Since the city is located on the edges of the Bay of Bengal, it became an important point of trade for the British, the French, and the Dutch, as they started trading in ivory, tobacco, muslin, and other products.

Once India gained independence in 1947, Visakhapatnam became one of the country's leading ports. It also hosts the seat of the Easter Naval Command of the Indian Navy.

This port city—also referred to as the Jewel of East Coast—is the administrative headquarters of the entire Visakhapatnam district and has recently become one of the most sought-out cities in India regarding tourism.

But we cannot mention Visakhapatnam and not mention the rich Buddhist history of the region. Recent archaeological excavations show that during King Ashoka's rule, the city was home to thousands of Buddhists and that Ashoka took Buddhism as a way toward Enlightenment.

Regarding the present day, Hinduism is the most widely followed religion here, followed by Islam and Christianity, showcasing how diverse this region is and the entirety of Southern India.

Furthermore, the city was nominated as one of the top 20 fastest-growing cities per the United Nations, giving it the impression of a modern silhouette overlooking a historic façade.

But, at this point, let's take a short break from India's anthropological and historical timeline and delve into one of the country's most important and defining social aspects—an art form that unites the entirety of India: movies!

As we already know, the movie industry is majorly dominated by Bollywood. But the actual industry that is more contextual and cultural here is often overlooked but is of immense importance as well. Perhaps you've heard of it? It's called Tollywood!

Tollywood is the informal term used to refer to the "Telugu" film industry, based in the Southern Indian states of Andhra Pradesh and Telangana. It is the second-largest film industry in India after Bollywood. The name "Tollywood" is a portmanteau of the words "Telugu" and "Hollywood."

Since it is such a huge part of the local Indian culture, it is bound to have a history as old as India. The industry dates to the early 1900s. The first Telugu film, "Bhakta Prahlada," was released in 1931. Since then, the industry has become India's major cultural and entertainment force. Tollywood produces around 200-250 films every year, with a market share of approximately 30% of the entire film market of India.

But one might ask, how is Tollywood different from Bollywood? Why is there a need for two separate film industries in the first place? Well, one of the defining characteristics of Tollywood is its emphasis on family-centric films.

Unlike Bollywood, which often focuses on action, romance, and drama, Tollywood films are known for their emphasis on familial relationships, particularly between parents and children. The movies often feature large ensemble casts and explore love, sacrifice, and redemption themes.

Naturally, these themes resonate with the general Indian population, hence the popularity and demand. Also, people find the industry a fresh change they need every so often from Bollywood.

Tollywood has produced some of the biggest stars in Indian cinema, including N. T. Rama Rao, Chiranjeevi, Nagarjuna, Venkatesh, Mahesh Babu, and Prabhas. These actors are household names in India and have a massive following in the Telugu-speaking states.

The Telugu film industry has also been at the forefront of technological advancements in Indian cinema. Tollywood was the first Indian film industry to introduce sound, and it has also been a pioneer in the use of computer-generated imagery (CGI) and other visual effects. In some sense, Bollywood may be more mainstream, but it is still a brainchild of the efforts of this industry.

But think not of it as a local phenomenon anymore because, in recent years, Tollywood has been expanding its global reach. Telugu films are now being released in markets outside India, including the United States, the United Kingdom, and the Middle East. The industry has also attracted investment from international players, including major studios like Walt Disney and Fox Star Studios.

In short, it is a vibrant and thriving film industry with a rich history and a bright future. With its focus on family-centric films and technological innovation, it has become an integral part of the Indian entertainment landscape and a major player on the global stage.

The vibrant and diversity-based films truly reflect India's soul in the most artistic manner possible.

CHAPTER 15:

CROWN OF THE WEST

It's that time when we take a short break from the East and head West, for this front of the country still has much more to show than meets the eye. Let's head to the Western Coast of India, bordered to the North-West by its neighbor, Pakistan.

Here resides, encompassing the entirety of the Kathiawar Peninsula, the famed and age-old city of Gujrat. Perhaps a city currently regarded as a symbol of diversity is also a historical relic. This is probably one of the subcontinent's oldest and most longstanding cities.

Its history begins in the Bronze Age settlements such as the Indus Valley civilization, where the coastal regions of Gujrat served as major ports and bustling trading centers.

This is something that we can clearly see as a constant in this place. Gujrat has, and always will, served its harboring functions for ships and docks. And today, much like in ancient civilizations, it is also a major business and commerce center.

It is also interesting to note that the state was powerful enough once to serve independently. After the fall of the Gupta Civilization, Gujrat flourished for many years as an independent Buddhist-Hindu state.

After that, it saw a shift in control to different rulers and dynasties, including the Gurjara-Pratihara Empire, Chaulukya Kingdom, the Delhi Sultanate, and the Gujarat Sultanate until it eventually got consolidated under the Mughal Empire during the early modern period.

Here Gujrati ports reached a new height of importance with the arrival of the East India Company. The region of Surat here became a breaking point for the oceanic trade between Europe and the Orient, and a factory was also established here in 1612.

By the time the last Mughal Emperor, Aurangzeb, came around, the Mughal Empire was knee-deep in religious and territorial conflict, which became evident in the consolidation of power in Gujrat.

After Aurangzeb's death, the Maratha nobles in Gujrat became even more powerful, and eventually, towns in the South, North, and central regions of the area came under their control. This eventually turned into another major shift in power in the face of the formation of the Maratha Empire.

However, during the colonial period, Gujrat was placed under the administration of the Bombay Presidency, which was controlled by the British themselves. The region was further subdivided into multiple princely states as well.

But these very people of Gujrat were also at the forefront of the Indian struggle for independence with leaders such as Mahatma Gandhi and Jawaharlal Nehru. These people included an array of different ethnicities and religions, and this diversity transcended to modern-day Gujrat as well.

Currently, the people of Gujrat, referred to as Gujrati, mostly speak the common language known to all, also called Gujarati. The population is a mix of colors with people from different religious and cultural backgrounds. These include Hindus, Muslims, Jain minorities, and the Bhil tribes.

The vibrant and diverse melting pot of cultures here is evident in many areas. Gujrat's art and craft industry embodies the intricate designs local to this region, with products such as the patola saree, table mats, quilts, cushions, and bed covers.

The folk Gujarati music and dance performances, are some things that are a sight for the entire country as people flock from far wide places to attend such festivals and displays which showcase forms such as Dandiya, Garba, and Padhar.

The dressing of this region also speaks of its identity. The Patola Silk, or "Queen of all Silks," is a major part of Gujratti attire and is commonly seen on Gujrati brides. The use of tie-dye and block prints is also quite common here. Chania Cholis are popular during festive seasons, and the Kediya dress is also for men.

But remember, as I said previously, there is more to the West than meets the eye, and that is where the modern aspect of it comes into play. If we move just to the South Western coast of India, we will find ourselves in the famous state of Goa.

Whenever people think of sunny days and sandy beaches, they imagine exotic islands like the Bahamas and Mauritius, but here, right in the Western heart of India, lies this state that matches these very exotic definitions and is known to cater to tourists from not only India but from all around the world.

If looking for a vacation spot in India to relax and unwind on pristine white beaches and clear blue waters, one must look no further than Goa. This entire state is known for this and the plethora of resorts, seafood, nightlife, and thrilling watersports that it offers.

This makes it a great spot for social and private events. It is the perfect honeymoon location, a great road trip with friends, an exciting holiday spot with family, and a place for some well-needed personal expeditions.

The Northern District of Goa is known for its lively and crowded beach life, with places such as Candolim, Anjuna, Baga, and Calangute. On the other hand, South Goa is known for much more quitter and calm beaches like Butterfly, Polem, and Angoda. Beach huts, luxury resorts, hot air balloon services, bird watching, scuba diving, sea rafting, and many other naturistic activities are part of the vibrant culture here.

Angoda Beach is perhaps the most famous sport here, and it is renowned for not just taking a dip in the water but also for its boat rides and the view it offers of the beauty of the nearby exquisite beaches of Butterfly and Honeymoon.

However, Visakhapatnam offers much more than just its breathtaking beaches. Like many other destinations in India, the state is adorned with remnants of antiquity. Forts like Aguada and Chapora exemplify this, concealing their ancient architectural splendor beneath the allure of the vast ocean and lush foliage.

Naturally, the state's geographical location offers it a lot of economic and political importance in the country. The tourism industry, as mentioned, is booming here all year round, but industrial sectors such as fishing and agriculture are also equally important here. This means that the region does extremely well on the socio-economic front post of the country, making it not only a great place to live but to invest and start a business as well.

This boom of lifestyle, culture, history, and economics obviously makes this relatively small state a golden ticket in the eyes of politics which is why the race to win a political seat in Goa is often tough and requires a major push of campaigning and trust-gaining.

So ask yourself.

Are you in the mood for a good tour through the ancient corridors of India? Or do you want to relax on a soft, sunny beach? Do you want to take your loved ones out on holiday? Are you in the mood for some good fish and shrimp? Do you enjoy nightlife and parties?

Regardless of what the answer is, depending on your mood, Goa has all the answers for you!

CHAPTER 16:

A JOURNEY FROM MAHARASHTRA TO RAJHASTAN

When we talk about the uniqueness of India, we will find that in all aspects of the country, it has something different to offer from the rest of the world. Take Maharashtra, for example; its geographical location differs from other subcontinent regions.

Maharashtra is a peninsular region located on the Western side of India on the Deccan Plateau. The Arabian Sea borders it to the West, the Indian states of Goa and Karnataka to the South, Telangana to the South-East, Chhattisgarh to the East, Madhya Pradesh and Gujrat to the North, and the union territory of Dadra and Nagar Haveli and Daman and Diu to the North-West.

That is one interesting form of geography. In simple language, it would mean that this area is mostly surrounded by water owing to the Arabian Sea, but the rest is bordered by the strips of land mentioned above. But the uniqueness does not simply end there; the place offers many more interesting facts.

According to accounts, approximately 52,000 years ago, a colossal meteor struck the Earth, imprinting its mark on some part of the planet's surface. Well, this mark is nowhere but our very own Maharashtra. You will find it in the form of the mysterious Lonar Lake, the only saline soda lake on Earth created due to this meteor.

Let's look at something else that might shock you. There is a village in this state which goes by the name of Shani Shingnapur. But what makes this place so different? It's a small thing, but it speaks volumes. If you walk through the small and colorful neighborhoods here, you will notice that the houses here have no doors! That's right, no entries whatsoever.

The people residing here firmly believe that whoever tries to steal anything will face the wrath of the God Shani Maharaj. And that keeps thieves at bay. But that also speaks of the people living in this state as a whole, which is why it is unsurprising that Maharashtra has the highest number of taxpayers in the country.

Another interesting fact: there is a village named Shetpal where each house had a separate resting place for live cobras in the rafters of their ceiling. It might sound dangerous, I understand. But to this day, there has been no case of a single cobra bite in that village. The wild animal lives in harmony with the villagers as their pets.

Your mind might be boggling with these seemingly surreal aspects of this state, so that I will leave you with one more thing. I'm sure you have played badminton at least once in your life. Well, it is believed that badminton was invented in this state, in the city of Pune, during British rule. The world-renowned sport we know today was once called "Poonah" here, named after the town.

The one thing locals popularly associate with Maharashtra is the food you can get here. The people here are extremely proud of their culture and ethos, which is well-reflected in the dishes. One traditional dish here is known as the Puran Poli, which is a type of Indian flat bread made by stuffing the bread made out of wheat flour with chickpeas, coconut, cane sugar, and nutmeg powder, which leaves a burst of sweet flavors on one's palette.

Then there is the Misal Pav, referred to as the king of street food here. It is made from Pav, which is an Indian bread roll, and Misal, which is a spicy curry made of moth beans. Often topped with coriander leaves and lemon, this dish is usually served with a glass of buttermilk.

If you want something to enjoy with your evening tea, look no further than Pudachi Vadi, which is a mixture of dried coconuts, coriander leaves, chili powder, and other Indian spices that are filled into a coating of gram flour and deep fried till it's golden brown—a perfect companion for tea.

The best combination of sweet and savory here is perhaps Keri Aamti which is a combination of a sweet and spicy gravy made from raw mangoes and Indian spices that is served over a bed of white rice. The fiery scent of the herbs and the tanginess of the mangoes pair in an unusually delicious harmony.

Then there is also Lord Ganesh's favorite snack that you will find here during festivals in various flavors, such as chocolate, pistachios, and kesar, and it is called Modak. The Kothimbir Vada is a healthy street dish made by mixing coriander leaves with besan and water, and Indian spices to give it a cake-like structure. It is served with spicy chilly and mint chutney.

We also cannot forget about the prince of street food here, the dish that Maharashtrians live for, a dish whose relationship with the people here can only be understood once it touches the tip of one's tongue. We are talking about the one and only Pav Bhaji.

I'm sure that by this point, water is drooling in your mouth, as in mine, so let's pause here and talk about a different land now. This state resides in northern India and is the largest state. Not only that, it is also the seventh-largest Indian state by population. We are talking about the Land of the Kings—Rajhastan. The name of this state is quite literally derived from the word "king."

This is quite an ancient piece of land as parts constituted the Indus Valley civilization, the Harrapan Civilization, the Matsya Kingdom of the Vedic Civilization, and many others. Different civilizations and states at some point in South Asian history have found their roots in this state, so naturally, we can expect much diversity from this place in terms of religion, culture, and, of course, history.

This is true and evident in the diverse communities that live here. We have the Rajputs who derive their name from the state's name. These usually consist of the wealthy upper class, business people, landlords, and in ancient times, warriors and soldiers.

Then there are the Jats, who constitute about 13 percent of the population. Jats are strong people in terms of strength and character. This is evident as they were also known to participate in the First and Second World Wars on behalf of British India. The dhoti and turban are two important dressing markers for Jat men, and the ghagra is one for women.

Then there are the Brahmans, considered the highest caste in Rajhastan, constituting over 12.5 percent of the population. They include many categories, such as Mahajans, who are known for trade, Vyas, who are the priests; then the Aboits, who are the temple caretakers; and others, such as Bhutia, Paliwals, and Saraswats. Most Brahmans would be found following priesthood, meaning they consume only vegetarian food.

There is also the Meena tribe here, considered one of the first tribes to settle in Rajhastan. Similarly, there is the Bhil tribe which is regarded as the largest tribe here, and in ancient times, they were considered great archers. The popular Ghoomar dance is an important and distinguishing part of their culture.

Then there is a caste called the Vaishya, known for their excellent trading and merchandise skills, which is why they also served as the financiers of Mughal emperors. The Chhipa community living here are the artisans who introduced the popular block print style to the region. There is also the Banjara tribe which is a very diverse nomadic tribe.

All these communities differ vastly from one another, yet they live in perfect harmony within the state, giving Rajhastan its unique colors of diversity. This wonderful cultural unity is partly due to different communities' religious tolerance.

The predominant religion here is Hinduism, and several folk heroes are worshipped here whose shrines can be seen all over the state. Islam is also majorly practiced here, with the shrine of one of the great Sufi scholars, Khwaja Moinuddin Chisti, residing here. Jainism is another widely followed religion, which is majorly practiced in temples such as Ossian Jain Temples, Dilwara Jain Temples, and Ranakpur Jain Temples.

Another important sect here is Dadupanthi, who follow the teachings of "Dadu," who preached notions like the equality of men, vegetarianism, celibacy, and abstinence from alcohol. There has been a major increase in the population of Sikhs living here as well. Christians also form a small minority within the population.

This unity is also evident in the different cultural practices that dominate Rajhastan. The "Attithi Devo Bhavo" is an important part of Rajasthani culture, and it refers to treating one's guests like they would treat God. This is why hospitality is an important part of Rajasthani culture. There is extreme joy and diversity in the folk music here as well.

The people here perform "ragas" for different purposes, such as to call forth rain or good sustenance. Traditional instruments such as sarangi, dhols, kamayach, and shehnai are used well. Folk songs revolve around different themes such as weddings, birth, and telling stories of romance and bravery.

There is color all around the place—from the religions to the folk songs—and it is the perfect expression of the region and the people that live in it. They are colorful in all aspects of life.

CHAPTER 17:

COLORFUL CELEBRATIONS OF NAGAR HAVELI

We have talked about both the states of Gujrat and Maharashtra. But there is something else that resides in between. Located in Wester, India, wedged between these two states lies a district that was once a defacto-free state but is now a Union territory known as Dadra and Nagar Haveli.

This is part of the larger Union territory collectively known as Dadra, Nagar Haveli, Daman, and Diu. The serene waters of the Daman Ganga River flow through this place as one part of the many tributaries of the mainstream Ganga as it peacefully enters the Arabian Sea.

The culture at Nagar Haveli comprises a fusion of what India generally has and a certain alienation of its tribal practices—bizarre and beautiful. It is a mix of mainstream cultures and those of the tribes—a functional, ethereal mix.

The tribal communities here, such as the Dublas, Koli, Kathodi, Naika, and Varlies, have rightfully preserved their cultural and ethnic practices. Some popular festivals include the Tarpa, Divasol, Akhtarij, Nariyeli, Purnima, and Monsoon Magic.

The distinct feature of each of these festivals is the renowned tribal dances. A famous one is the Bhawada Dance, in which the Kokna tribespeople wear masks depicting local God and Goddesses and dance with their feet and hips to traditional Indian beats.

The Tarpa dance is mainly performed by the Varli, Kokna, and Koli tribes of Dadra and Nagar Haveli. The dance, usually performed on moonlit nights, reflects the unity of these tribes as they swing in circles and sing to the rhythm of the instrument called "Tarpa" until past midnight.

There is also the Tur and Thali dance, popularly performed at weddings and other special occasions by the Dublas and Dhodis tribe members and women who dance to the beats of *dhol* and other instruments as they arrange in circles and clap their hands along the beat.

The arts and handicrafts of this area are also particular to the people here. Dadra and Nagar Haveli artisans are known to construct handcrafted bamboo baskets, leather items, bamboo mats, and carvings on tortoiseshells and ivory. There are also the Warli paintings which are a significant part of local marriages as people believe them to possess divine powers.

There are other separate practices of these tribes, adding to the region's richness. The Barash is a tribal festival celebrated by the Kokna and Varli communities during Diwali. The Dhodias celebrate the Divaso festival to evoke the Goddess Kali's good spirit during crop harvesting. The Kokhna tribe celebrates a festival called Akha Tij, which is specific to the women of that community.

However, there is more to adore about this place than just its rich culture. Nestled between two prominent states, this district possesses a beauty that is uniquely its own—timeless and pristine. The Vangana Lake is a peaceful spot flowing through lush green gardens adorned with exotic flowers and other flora.

Long ago, this area was under the control of Portuguese traders, and the relics of that are still all around the place. The Our Lady of Piety

Church was built around 1887 and is a splendid display of Portuguese architectural prowess.

The icing on the cake is the sight of lions lazing around casually at the Safari Wildlife Park. These Asiatic beasts have been preserved from hunting and other destructive activities of human life and live peacefully in the serenity and comfort of these green lands.

It also hosts the exotic Zodiac flower spread all over the Nakshatra Garden in the capital city of Silvassa. The Daman Ganga also receives its fair share of tourists visiting the Madhuban Dam who enjoy water activities such as water scooter rides, bumper boat rides, water gliding, and speed boat rides.

Much like Dadra and Nagar Haveli, richness is spread throughout Daman and Diu. The people of Daman and Diu are known for their hospitable character. They are warm, friendly, open to tourists, and enjoy all seasons.

Much like Dadra and Nagar Haveli, the people here are known to follow old traditions and customs but are very open to allowing tourists to explore their lands and culture and understand more about them. This includes their local art, music, literature, and folklore.

They perform traditional dances on various occasions, such as marriages, death, good harvest, and monsoon. Special costumes are also designed for different festivals. Costumes of Daman and Diu are influenced by Gujarati traditions and those of the Portuguese (who once controlled these lands). These include the Ghagra blouse and the Odhani.

Since there is a bustling Hindu population in these areas intermingling with Muslims and Christians, one will see different festivals celebrated year-round. This includes Makarshankranti—which is a Hindu observance—in January and Christmas and New Year's Eve in December. Holy, Diwali, and Eid are other popular festivals celebrated here with a burst of energy and activity. Gangaji Fair is held every year at the Somnath Mahadev Temple in Daman. Purnima is also an important festival that marks the beginning of the fishing season. The Parsees have their Parsi New Year celebrations.

If one truly wishes to see the intermingling of different cultures, ethnicities, religions, and people sharing each other's happiness, there is no better place to visit than this little district of enormous cultural wealth.

CHAPTER 18:

THE GRAND CITIES OF THE EAST

Spread linearly across the banks of the Hooghly River, the city is known for its grand colonial architectural design, art, galleries, and cultural festivals. Kolkata is in the Eastern part of India and is the capital of the State of West Bengal.

Everything about this city resonates with grandiosity, elegance, and glamour. It is unsurprising because this is what the state's history offers. Back in the colonial era, Kolkata (formerly Calcutta) was *the* British establishment and was later declared the capital of British India.

Its history as a British settlement started when Job Charnock established a trading post in 1690 on behalf of the English East India Company. This place was well protected back then as it is now. With the cover of the Hooghly River on the West, a creek to the North, and salt lakes to the East, Kolkata was the strategic juggernaut for trading and protection from British rivals, such as the Dutch and the Portuguese.

Additionally, the local villages of Sutanati, Kalikata, and Gobindapore were already popular with Indian merchants, establishing Kolkata as a good place for commerce. In 1698, the English embarked on their colonial journey as they received permits that gave them the privilege of purchasing zamindari (land) rights in this region.

Freedom of private trade was also granted by the Mughals in 1717 to the company, which meant that more merchants flocked to the area, and many company servants started conducting duty-free private trade.

As British rule expanded in the State of Bengal, the remnants of the Mughal Dynasty, under the banner of Nawab Siraj ud Daulah, attempted to regain their former glory; he sacked Kolkata. John Holwell and some other Europeans who were defending it were captured.

The capture of Caucasians gave birth to the infamous Black Hole prison system. It was the harshest imprisonment, where the criminal was sentenced to solitary confinement at 252 square feet (18 feet x 14 feet). The prison cell had no window and, therefore, no sunlight. After a while, imprisoned people would not know whether it was the day outside or not.

The Nawab imprisoned Europeans in the local jail for petty offenses. Historians believe that in such a small prison cell, 64 prisoners were incarcerated, and more than 20 died.

In a stunning turn of events, the Nawab suffered a decisive defeat in the Battle of Plassey in 1757. Consequently, the British regained control of Kolkata, firmly establishing their dominion over Bengal. Then, in 1772, Warren Hastings, the Inaugural Governor General of British India, orchestrated a momentous shift. He relocated the entire administrative apparatus from Murshidabad to Kolkata, effectively transforming Fort William into the nerve center of British governance.

The flourishment of Kolkata as the capital continued throughout the 1800s. Railways were constructed, and inland customs duties were abolished, creating an open market for trading. The Grand Trunk Road from Kolkata to Peshawar (now in Pakistan) was completed to establish an even stronger connection between the two cities. British banking, insurance, and mercantile interests flourished, and Kolkata became the busy commercial hub we know today.

Now, if one visits Kolkata, one must spend some time getting accustomed to the architectural and historical richness of the city and pay tribute to all the relics of the past. We cannot start this conversation without mentioning the pristine marble beauty of the Victoria Memorial Hall.

This museum is perhaps one of India's most popular tourist destinations, where people from the city and worldwide visit to witness the extravagance of the building itself and all the tokens of colonial history that it guards inside.

The grandly-lit iconic landmark, named the "Howrah Bridge," connects Kolkata to the city of Howrah. Its eye-catching magnificence is nothing short of the Golden Gate Bridge itself. This city also fashions the tomb of one of the greatest humanitarians ever. Mother House is a serene monument with an ambiance as calm as the person whose tomb and chapel are built inside—Mother Teresa.

If one wishes to experience what the British saw in this area and walk down a lane of legacy as they did, there is no better place to visit than the street in front of the Victorian Memorial Hall, which is known as Park Street. You will find everything the British liked about the place—bustling merchandise, crowds, stalls, restaurants—here.

A humbling reminder of the British Raj and the prevalence of nationalism stands in South Park Street in the form of old tombs and monuments established by the British colonials—the South Park cemetery. There is also the living embodiment of the dream of Bishop Daniel Wilson, who commissioned the construction of Saint Paul's Cathedral here in 1847. The towering monument of white marble is still an important Christian center.

There is also a popular street known as Boi Para or College Street, which is regarded as the Wonder of Kolkata. It is said that walking here would make one feel the very 200-year-old essence of Kolkata. It is a paradise for book lovers who can find all sorts of genres here, from academics to history to fiction to non-fiction to art and poetry.

There is also the iconic Eden Garden, the largest cricket stadium in India, and it has hosted many matches in various international and national competitions throughout the years. However, Kolkata is so much more than just a cosmopolitan center and a relic of history.

Back in the day, Kolkata was home to not just Chinese and Anglo-Indian communities but also European and Eurasian ones, along with the Dutch. Such diversity is evident in the modern day too. While Bengalis dominate the population demographic, the city is home to many Hindus and Muslims. There are many Urdu speakers, as well as Odia, Gujarati, Punjabi, Nepali, and English-speaking minorities as well.

Nevertheless, this feature—a burst of different ethnicities and a trip to the past—is also evident in other cities of Eastern India. There is grandiosity associated with this entire region of the country. Such is evident in the city of Puri.

Puri is a coastal city found in the municipality of Odisha state on the Bay of Bengal. It is popularly regarded as the "Temple City" for it hosts the Jagannath Temple, which is a remark of one of the four original pilgrimage sites for Hindus.

The temple is an important building for Hindus and is dedicated to Jagannath, who is a form of Lord Vishnu. The Somavamsa King originally built the temple, which has been rebuilt in the past ten centuries. The temple is famous for the annual Ratha Yatra, or the chariot festival, which witnesses a flock of pilgrims and tourists from all over the country.

The temple is a sacred and holy site, not to mention one of architectural magnificence. Furthermore, it is said that many Vaishnava (which is a Hindu caste) saints were associated with its walls. There are many legends and folk tales about the temple's origins, making it of immense importance to historians, archaeologists, and anthropologists alike.

Regardless of how you look at such areas of Eastern India, a glimpse into history, or a vision of the diversity of today, it is still a marvelous remarkable sight and a wonderful reflection of the country as a whole.

CHAPTER 19:

DIVERSITY IN BHUBANESHWAR

The capital and the largest city of the Indian State of Odisha, Bhubaneshwar, also known as the 'Temple City,' owing to the seven-hundred temples that once stood here, is in the eastern coastal plains along the axis of the Eastern Ghats Mountain range.

Much like other cities of India, this region is bound and rooted by rivers. To the south flows the Data River, and to the east is the Kuakahi River. Interestingly, the Chandaka Wildlife Sanctuary and the Nandan Kanan Zoo lie in the western and northern regions of the city. So, you can expect much lush greenery in this area!

An interesting fact about this place is that it is considered relatively modern, adding a contemporary touch to all the ancient corridors of India. The city was formally established in 1948, right after the partition.

However, just because it was formally inaugurated as a city in 1948 does not mean it lacks rich cultural and historical nuances. The present-day area can be dated back to the 7th century. With Puri and Konark, two other famous temple-centric cities, Bhubaneshwar forms the "Golden Triangle," making these three places the most visited sites in India.

The city itself has a vibrant cultural heritage, and it is believed that some temples here even date back to the 6th and 11th centuries! This makes it a long-standing place of worship and spiritual importance for the people of the subcontinent.

One such example of a temple is the most famous and often-visited one here, which is known as the Ekamra Kshetra. The Ekamra Kshetra is not a temple in itself; it contains a series of unique temple-like architectural monuments, making it a temple complex.

The city is also home to the famous Lingaraj Temple, which is dedicated to the Hindu deity of Shiva. Other prominent sacred sites include the Mukteswara Temple, Rajrani Temple, and the Ananta Temple.

This is not just an architectural monument but an important and active place of worship. It attracts devotees from all over India who come here to witness important religious ceremonies and vibrant festivals. This is why during celebrations such as Maha Shivaratri, Ratha Yatra, and Durga Puja, the temple complex is a remarkable sight in itself!

Much like any other place in India, the rich culture is well reflected in the people's vibrancy and activities. There is great diversity in the types of languages spoken here. Mainly people use the local language of Oriya but other than that, you will also find the locals speaking Assamese and Bengali.

As mentioned before, festivals are a huge part of the culture here, which is why they are celebrated with great joy and ecstasy, but they also emphasize local art, crafts, and music. This is why fairs such as Adivasi Mela, Toshali National Crafts Mela, and Rajdhani Book Fair are popular.

If you visit the streets of Bhubaneshwar, check out the famous rice and fish curry called "Maccha Jholo" in the local language. One should also try out the sweets here, such as Rasabali, Chenna Poda, and Roshogolia.

Since we have previously talked about the temple city of Puri and Bhubaneshwar, it would be nothing short of an injustice not to discuss the third piece of this triangular puzzle, Konark.

Konark is a town located in the Puri district in the state of Odisha. Like Puri, it lies on the Bay of Bengal, 65 kilometers from Bhubaneshwar. It hosts the great 13th century Sun Temple, also known as Black Pagoda, a UNESCO World Heritage Site.

Despite mostly being in ruins, this beautiful architectural marvel is built mainly out of black granite and still sees a flock of visitors, tourists, and devotees. It had also given the region its name because Konarka is derived from the Sanskrit word 'Kona' and 'Arka,' which together a reference to the temple, which was dedicated to the Sun God.

The temple's remains appear to be a 100-foot-high chariot with an immense wheel carved out of stone, all a reference to the Hindu Sun God, Surya. And much like Bhubaneshwar and Puri, it shares the rich history and culture of the state.

One such example is the classical Odissi dance which was completely forgotten in the British colonial era but revived once again after Indian independence and became popular here in Konark. Moreover, the region has also regained knowledge of other forms of local dances such as the Chhau dance, which is a tribal martial dance, the Mahari dance, which was performed by women belonging to the Devadasi cult, and the Gotipua as well.

Literature and arts have been an important part of the culture of Konark. The region is known to have produced great poems and epic folk tales, some of which date back to 900 AD. Local shops host the works of the people living here, with displays of beautiful applique artwork, delicate silver filigree work, palm leaf painting, and sand sculptures. Konark is also famous for its handloom sarees, such as Bandha, Bomkai, Ikat, and Pasapalli.

The temple, much like its name, gives light and meaning to the social order of this region. It is a reminder of the strength and stability of what was once known as the 'Ganga Empire.' Its divine aura connects people to their spiritual roots and blesses all their daily wages, as it is popularly believed!

CHAPTER 20:

INDIA TODAY

Naturally, we arrive at the end of this magical and spiritual journey. As we glided through the holy waters of the Great Ganges, we came at the meander that flows gently and organically into the Arabian Sea, taking us with it. The river holds every droplet of the history of this enchanted place, and it gently pushes it, wave by wave, into the great sea, and the sea only pushes it back onto the beach as the tide rises.

Much like those droplets of history and culture, our journey should also come full circle, and it is only right to glimpse back at the façade of this extravagant land as it slowly disappears from our view and talk about the state that it is in today—the height of the post-modern world.

Let us first zoom out and take in the big picture and try to understand where India lies on the canvas of the entire world, where it stands, and how important it is to the rest of the human population. Naturally, a country hosting over 1.4 billion people becomes a target audience for business empires located in the rest of the world.

Therefore, global economies such as the United States see India as a lucrative destination for their products and services. This is also one of the reasons why India hosts multitudes of outsourced international businesses as well.

The next important question is this: where does the economy stand? The entire world market took a massive hit in the past few years owing to the Covid-19 pandemic, but India has experienced robust economic growth in recent years, and although the pandemic impacted the market severely here, India showed resilience and potential for long-term expansion. The country has a thriving middle class of different backgrounds that drives demand across various sectors, which naturally regulates economic supply and maintains a healthy balance.

Speaking of businesses and outsourcing, India is currently considered a global hub for information technology. The country is known for its highly skilled workforce and cost-effective services. Many multinational corporations outsource their IT and customer support functions to Indian companies, contributing to India's prominence in the global services industry.

India has witnessed a significant rise in entrepreneurial activities and a vibrant start-up ecosystem. The government has introduced initiatives such as "Startup India" to foster innovation and entrepreneurship. Indian start-ups have gained attention and investments from global venture capital firms, driving technological advancements and disruption across various sectors.

Cities like Bengaluru, often called India's Silicon Valley, are home to a vibrant community of tech entrepreneurs. Start-ups have gained recognition for their e-commerce, fintech, health tech, edtech, and agricultural tech innovations.

Let us not forget that India's name on the world map is undoubtedly there because of active government support. The Indian government has been implementing reforms to improve the ease of business, attract foreign direct investment (FDI), and stimulate economic growth. Initiatives such as the Goods and Services Tax (GST), Insolvency and Bankruptcy Code (IBC), and liberalization of FDI policies demonstrate India's commitment to creating a conducive business environment.

We must not forget that it is not entirely perfect from an economic standpoint since the country does face challenges such as infrastructure gaps, bureaucratic procedures, and socio-economic disparities. However, the country's immense potential, market size, and ongoing reforms make it a crucial player in the current foreign market landscape.

It is also important to mention that modernity in India has brought a lot of influence on Western trends and cultures that often seem to be prioritized more by people in urban areas over local trends. However, the spirit of India remains tight in the hands of those who embody the country's soul.

Western fashion trends have gained more popularity among the younger generation. Western-style clothing, including casual, formal, and street fashion, has entered the Indian wardrobe. Another area where this is evident is the entertainment and media industry; Hollywood movies and music genres have a huge following in India and directly impact Indian pop culture.

Another area where this is evident is the mass increase in Western-style urban dining areas; pizzas, burgers, and café culture are more than common in India now. Learning and speaking English, as a global lingua franca has become extremely common in Indian society, especially using English terms and phrases in local languages.

Western trends of openness and normality of dating culture are often looked at negatively by certain locals due to age-old norms; however, such influences have also brought normalcy and inclusion for marginalized groups such as the LGBTQI+ community. In 2018, the Supreme Court passed a landmark resolution decriminalizing consensual same-sex relations by striking down Section 377 of the Indian penal code.

Normality and openness bring vulnerability which has been another positive thing for the Indian youth, which has become increasingly aware of and sensitive towards mental health issues such as anxiety and depression which were often overlooked in the traditional Indian culture. This allows the population, especially the youth, to mentally strive for the best, which is why India currently produces the highest number of physicians and engineers globally.

Bollywood has also been a juggernaut in Indian success worldwide since Bollywood films have taken huge strides in displaying the rich Indian cultural heritage, traditions, and diversity globally. Actors like Shahrukh Khan is not just Indian sensation, but he is a heartthrob all around the world and one of the world's highest-paid actors. Bollywood plays a major role in influencing global fashion trends and music interests, with its esteemed actors and actors serving as style icons.

Overall, it would be an understatement to say that the people of this rich and beautiful nation have come a long way ever since they struggled for independence in 1947. The nation's leaders strengthened this country's initial foundations and gave the people living here a unanimous identity, regardless of their religion, sex, color, creed, and caste.

Their eyes would gleam with joy and pride to see how far we have come in advancing the vision of Bharat that they dreamed of—the concept of beauty, diversity, charm, and extravagance!

I hope you had as much fun journeying through this mystical land as I had writing about it!

NOTE FROM THE AUTHOR

The history of South Asia, in particularly the subcontinent and India, has seen a lot of tumult and turbulence in the last couple of centuries leaving behind a rich tapestry for the generations to inherit—one that is filled with as much luster as it is with blood.

Welcome to India is all about healing and looking at this heavy ancestry from a fresh, modern lens where we take a journey to explore our culture, history, architecture, and diversity in great depth, looking through the kaleidoscope of colors that is our land—the way it was meant to be seen.

Sit back as I take you on a journey through the vast corridors of India where we explore not just the ever-changing geography and physicality of the region, but also the constantly growing and evolving cultures and array of people.

It is a testament to the beauty of India, and her people.

www.ingramcontent.com/pod-product-compliance
Lightning Source LLC
Chambersburg PA
CBHW040728120726

48010CB00001B/55